GOD ON THE STARTING LINE

Other books by Marc Bloom

Cross Country Running

The Marathon

Olympic Gold

The Runner's Bible

The Know Your Game Series

The Miler

Run with the Champions

GOD
ON THE
STARTING LINE

The Triumph of a Catholic School
Running Team and Its Jewish Coach

Marc Bloom

BREAKAWAY BOOKS
HALCOTTSVILLE, NEW YORK
2007

God on the Starting Line: The Triumph of a Catholic School Running Team and Its Jewish Coach

ISBN: 978-1-891369-74-2
Library of Congress Control Number: 2007925649

Published by Breakaway Books
P.O. Box 24
Halcottsville, NY 12438
(800) 548-4348
www.breakawaybooks.com

FIRST PAPERBACK EDITION

For

Michael Dunn

Justin Gallagher

Ryan Lavender

John Lennon

John Leschak

Chris Ruhl

Brock Silvestri

Michael Solebello

—champions all—

and their families

Contents

Foreword

Just about every moving experience I've had in running—from accompanying my wife, Andrea, in the New York City Marathon (it was she who wound up talking about it on *Good Morning America*) to following my daughters, Allison and Jamie, in their running pursuits (alternately getting in the way and thrilling to their hard-won successes) to observing Eamonn Coghlan in Dublin as he trained to become the first forty-year-old to run a sub-four-minute mile (yes, he did it, at age forty-one in 1994)—has found its way into print. So when I started coaching the St. Rose High School cross-country team, at first struggling to motivate the boys or even get their attention, I started keeping notes because I figured, there must be a story here somewhere. I couldn't know then that coaching the Running Roses would become the most affecting story of all.

As the boys got stronger and grew into championship contenders, my scribblings filled a ream of paper and I wrote a short piece about the team in *Runner's World* magazine. The reaction was terrific. Readers responded to my themes of striving and humanity, and came up to me at running events to discuss the coach-athlete relationship. They referred to the boys by name. I decided then to expand the article into this book. For me, writing about the team was as moving as the coaching itself.

I must thank the boys' parents for giving me that chance: for embracing me, supporting their sons and seeing the value in my approach. I also thank the fine people at St. Rose High School, in particular my colleague Bill Jasko, the girls' coach for a number of years who shared my passion for reaching the young runners.

I am grateful to the many friends and colleagues involved with Catholic teaching and running who offered relevant ideas. They include Bob Andrews, Brian Caulfield, Denis Ganey, Ed Grant, Jamie Kempton and Patrick O'Neill.

I also thank the editors at *Runner's World* and the *New York Times* sports department for enabling me to write on my favorite subject, Garth Battista of Breakaway Books for his editorial guidance, and my agent, Richard Curtis, for his faith in my work.

My wife, Andrea, my soul mate and role model as an extraordinary second-grade teacher, signed on to my running passions a long time ago. I don't think she knew what she was getting into. But it's been a beautiful ride together.

Marc Bloom
Marlboro, New Jersey

1

Boys of Summer

My boys arrive at the track, tan and freckled and plump, piling out of parents' cars with new running shoes and tentative smiles for the first day of summer cross-country practice. "Hi, Coach," they say, one after another. "Howyadoin', Coach." I like the sound of that. I'm not big on formality or titles, but I'm tickled to hear teenage boys call me Coach. I want them to feel they can rely on me. I want to come through for them. I want to come through for myself.

The late-June winds, cooling off in the evening hour, tip infield cones I've placed at the start and finish line. As the boys assemble, all four of them, I hurry to set the cones right. I like everything neat and in place. Symmetry and order give me a sense of control. My brown accordion folder, thick with files for meet schedules, results, rosters, injuries, media and course maps, sits regally on a bare gray grandstand bench. I carry a spiral notebook where I record the day's training and observations like how an athlete pushes the pace or capitulates to fatigue.

"What's the workout today, Coach?" says Justin Gallagher, hoping to coast.

"Got something tough today, Coach?" says Mike Solebello, wary but looking to be tested.

I wave off the parents who give up their sons to me for half a year, at an age when the boys are vulnerable and exposed. They want to be cool and accepted and can veer anywhere from obedient honor student to untamed rascal, from goal-setting athlete to bullied nerd who winds up—perish the thought—being a gun-toting headline on the evening news. As the father of two daughters, I have leaped into scary, uncharted male waters. Boys, to be honest, never held much appeal for me. Their scowls and macho acts and complex, hidden behaviors don't seem worth the effort.

But when I went looking for a coaching position four years ago, this is what I got: St. Rose High School in Belmar, New Jersey, a half-hour drive from home, three blocks from the beach on the Jersey Shore. I'd sent my résumé, brimming with three decades of writing about running, to every high school in Monmouth County. The one call I got came from the athletic director at St. Rose, a seventy-five-year-old coed Catholic school with 637 students. The Running Roses needed a boys' cross-country coach.

It was quite a letdown. The year before, I'd come *this* close to getting the girls' cross-country position at a nearby school that was bursting with excellent, eager runners. I knew the kids, met the parents at a coffee klatch as though I were running for local office, and had a sports connection in the district go to bat for me with the superintendent's office. Still, the bureaucracy prevailed. Even though my life's work revolved around young runners, a teacher in the school was chosen. I guess that made sense. I had never coached a team before.

After my daughters left for college, I wanted to coach girls. I wanted to be around girls' sweetness and smiles, their amiability. I

wanted to embrace their needs and help them excel. I felt a gnaw-
ing, desperate void when Allison and Jamie departed. Leaving my
younger daughter, Jamie, in Washington to get settled at school, I
experienced a thundering, onrushing dread, like nothing I'd ever
felt before. It caused me to burst out in a heaving, uncontrollable
wail, a tidal wave of emotion that uncovered succeeding waves of
emotion and made me look hard at how I dealt with intimacy and
separation. It took a therapist to help me sort out my feelings and
feel safe.

Now I'm okay but still lapse into vague fears having something
to do with lost innocence and the need—still—to nurture young
people and feel needed. I always feel better when I'm around my
boys, who do need me and show me that they do, like when Ryan
Lavender, a junior, tells me this evening at the track that he ran five
miles this morning even though we're training hard tonight.

Ryan's ambition is commendable but it can get the best of him.
His talent is of championship caliber but he squanders it. He must
learn to pace himself. Distance running is a game of patience: A
long, steady buildup, in which you absorb more and more stress, is
the way to train. Ryan, who starred two years ago as a freshman but
has sagged since, is my pet project. He nods his head yes when I
instruct him to start a race under control, but then he darts to the
front—right in the lead, daringly, like he can run away from the
field at will. But he can't, yet. I want to berate him after his reck-
lessness leads to defeat, but instead I grab him around the shoulders, hug the daylights out of him, and see if through my physical
touch something of my lesson will rub off.

Ryan's a tough case, all right. I still find out from his mother,
Karen, that Ryan did some knucklehead guy-thing, like run a half-
marathon just for the hell of it—despite my plea not to—and that's

the reason his Achilles tendon hurts. Karen will whisper this fact to me in exasperation, like, *You know stubborn Ryan, he does his own thing, there's nothing we can do about it.* Karen and her husband, Dennis, have gone through a bitter divorce, which illuminates the anger I detect in Ryan and makes me want to hug him even more. After practice, I will sit with him and talk. But he says little. He's a boy.

At least Ryan and the others follow the workouts I give them. In my first year of coaching, I was like a new teacher trying to holler the class into submission. St. Rose produces excellent teams, but the cross-country coaching job had been a revolving door, with faculty members doing little more than babysitting the squad for years. In 1997, I inherited a mostly senior group of wise guys who'd received no direction and spent most of practice imitating the professional wrestlers they'd seen on television. When I took over, they would quit and walk in the middle of runs and slack off at every opportunity. On even the hottest days, it was impossible to get anyone to bring a water bottle to practice. That would have signified compliance with authority. Who wants to be the first to crack and give in?

The one true runner I had thought he was too good for the team and practiced on his own. At a school meeting, his mother cornered me to complain that I was not training her son hard enough. I told her I'd be delighted to run the boy's legs off, if only he would show up.

The boy did appear at practice the day the seniors decided to fulfill an initiation rite. This was not a day to be missed. On the Jersey Shore boardwalk where we train after school, and out of my view, the older kids picked up a nerdy freshman, rushed down the beach, and tossed the boy into the ocean. I was incensed—after all, the boy could have drowned—but let the incident pass without punishment. Reluctant to reveal my lack of authority, I didn't want to make an issue out of the episode with school administrators. The soaking-wet freshman shrugged it off but later quit the team. So I sucked it up, plowing on with boys I felt I could coach and even like if I'd had them to mold when they entered the school. But now they were too world-weary to follow any rules from a neophyte like me.

The hardest worker that season was a lumbering six-foot-eight kid named Henry who was getting in shape for basketball. "Big Hank," I called him. Big Hank might have been the tallest cross-country runner in New Jersey. And he was probably the slowest. When tired, his torso would droop forward like an old man's, wasting energy and causing more fatigue. "Straighten up!" I'd call to Big Hank in races. He would until finally caving in altogether.

Another endearing boy that season was Rory, who had a stride so clean I called him "the Ethiopian," after the great runners from that country. Rory wasn't fast but the nickname seemed to motivate him and he would show up for practice waiting for me to say it: *Here comes the Ethiopian.* I learned that little things like that, which seem inconsequential, can count for a lot in reaching teenage boys. Rory could tell that I cared about him in a personal way, and he knew that I meant the moniker as a compliment. Even that small taste of camaraderie whet my appetite for more.

I thought about that recently when I spoke with a high school coach from Illinois, Joe Newton, whose teams from York High have won 20 state cross-country titles. In my work, I speak often with coaches of Newton's pedigree, devouring the way they transform reluctant teenage boys into committed runners. Newton told me that he developed crucial relationships with his team by giving each boy a nickname, in effect a caring identity. Years later at York reunions, said Newton, boys come up to him, saying, "Remember me? Meathead."

With my minuscule team of eight members, I must be careful to treat everyone the same. Kids despise favoritism and let you know it. If I crown one boy with a nickname, everyone has to get one. Unless there's a clearly distinguishable character, someone who sets himself apart, whom all the boys accept as a levitating personality. I have such a candidate. His name is John Lennon. And I call him Eleanor Rigby, Strawberry Fields, Penny Lane, but mostly Sgt. Pepper.

John loves the attention and eats it up. When one boy chirps up with an "Eleanor who?" John counters with, "The Beatles, you asshole." I pull John aside, not for the first time, and tell him I'm not going to tolerate language like that so watch your mouth. I'm stunned and embarrassed by the boys' coarse words expressed out in the open. I'm careful to watch my words in their presence but I don't want to make an issue out of every "fuck you" that I hear. I don't want cross-country to seem like school.

At St. Rose, where rigidity rules—some might call it "compassionate conservatism"—the boys get their marching orders daily. A crooked tie can result in after-school detention (and offers an excellent excuse to be late for practice). Lennon, a senior who is running reluctantly to get in shape for the baseball and basketball teams, leads the league in detention. He takes it in stride, as a badge of honor, anything to try to impress girls. Girls seem to like him, too; John's got a quick wit and a forward but nonthreatening come-on.

Even though he doesn't know beans about running, John's a good athlete and I need him. I see how he sticks his face into the wind, his brow furled, gutting out a hard run, denying pain. This kid can be a runner if he wants to. That's my job—to make him want to. So far, I'm failing miserably. After coming to a few practices as a freshman, John quit cross-country to play soccer. As a sophomore, he skipped fall sports. Last year, he joined the squad in midseason and was of little help. This year I've been on his case, feeding his ego, appealing to his senior-year responsibility to finally run a whole season. I will even give John permanent Sgt. Pepper status if that will work.

You never know what works. My high school coach in Brooklyn in the early sixties gave me a nickname. That didn't work. "C'mon, Bloom, blossom," he'd call as I huffed and puffed through a cross-country race. I never liked Blossom; it sounded too girlish. And I never would blossom, until I gave up the idea of being a great runner and started writing about those who would.

I think my writing has been rooted in teaching. In every story, I try to shed some light on what makes a competent runner. I need to know for myself. It's a never-ending search, a gathering of examples and prescriptions, with implicit lessons, I hope, that can help young people achieve. I want to rescue kids the way Holden Caulfield said he wanted to, when they're still pure and hopeful, and get them running, to find the way, or one way, to a meaningful life. To me, the answers in running are oftentimes the answers in life itself.

I consider teaching, coaching, broadly, as in the rabbinical sense of imparting a spiritual grounding, a sure and simple path to unleash the power all kids have to succeed. I think I could have been a rabbi. I could have been one of those "running rabbis" who finds the moving, sweaty body a worthy partner with the pulpit. As I learn more about faith, pounding my chest in prayer with God's devotion, I search for ways to make the St. Rose squad see the purifying link between hard work and life's blessings.

So far, I've rescued five boys who show signs of giving themselves to cross-country running, of having the will to be different: Michael Dunn, Justin Gallagher, Ryan Lavender, Brock Silvestri, and Michael Solebello. These are my boys, the heart of my team, all entering their junior year at St. Rose. We are growing together like a family and, as in almost any family, there is love and dysfunction, energy and listlessness, trust and betrayal. We make gains, lose a step, recover, struggle onward. We are a cross-country team.

We go against the grain, the masses, the culture of acquisition. As I recite in prayer on the Jewish Sabbath, there are times when we are called not to acquire but to share. Define *share* how you like. Treat people with kindness and respect and there's nothing you can't accomplish. The best high school coach I ever knew, Milt Blatt, who developed record-breaking squads at Andrew Jackson High in New York City a generation ago, once told me of his approach, "I treated the athletes as if they were young friends of mine."

But you can't start out that way. This much I learned when I taught English and creative writing in a New York middle school in the nineteen seventies. At the outset, I tried to be my students' buddy and they buried me. Then I became tough and demanding, earning their respect or at least their fear; after that, I could ease up and be their "friend." It's a process, and once you—teacher, coach— achieve that delicate balance of autocracy and warmth, it can be transcendent. When kids know you care and that they can rely on you, they will go beyond the highest standards. One writing class I taught was so in sync with my style that the students decided on their own to write a full-length play and perform it for the entire school. Instead of the yawns that usually greet class productions, these kids got raves.

I'm working toward that ideal with my boys at St. Rose. More than anything, I want them to take the initiative, to show they will work hard because it's important to them, not because I tell them to. We're not there yet; frankly, we're not even close.

Tonight, four of the eight boys show up and no incoming freshmen. "Where's Lennon?" I ask, but there are only shrugs. I want to say, *Where's that darn Lennon whom I've been doting on and calling every few weeks to see how he's doing in baseball, and who promised me he'd run this summer?* but I keep those protestations to myself. I can't help it, but this sport, these boys, this chance to create something with spiritual power drives me to relentless calculation and fussiness.

Sometimes I have to stop myself and remember what my former high school track teammate, Stu Levine, an accomplished coach, told me. Kids being raw and fertile, any running you give them will make them stronger, so don't fret over designer workouts. Just don't do anything that fouls a kid up. That makes sense. The problem is, I know that the coaches of the best teams, like Christian Brothers Academy, winner of five straight state cross-country titles and situated right down the road from my home, have a year-round system to find, keep, and train boys to run as if nothing else mattered.

I send my four athletes—Lavender, Silvestri, Solebello, and Gallagher—out on the school fields for a ten-minute warm-up run. I'm wary that a groundskeeper might order us away. St. Rose has no track and we are mooching off Marlboro High, where I live and my daughters went to school and ran on the Mustangs' cross-country team. I think that gives me some territorial rights.

When my daughter Allison ran, her coach, Maryanne Lippin, a marathon runner, insisted on discipline. If you were a minute late for summer practice at a park trail, Lippin and the team took off and you were left in the parking lot by yourself. Marlboro had one of the state's best teams. Same thing with Christian Brothers. Miss summer practice without notifying the coach, Tom Heath, and you can pack your bags, fella, you're out.

I have to plead, cajole, promise the world to get kids to run when they don't have to. This fall, I'm taking the team on its first out-of-town trip, to a meet in North Carolina. The event is in September, and the boys know they have to be in tip-top shape for the meet, which draws teams from all over the country. We don't want to be embarrassed. We've raised funds for our trip with a recent golf outing and are raising more money this summer through pledges for miles trained. If this doesn't motivate the guys to run, I don't know what will.

Summer practice is optional, a coach's prerogative, but essential for cross-country, a fall sport requiring hundreds of miles of preseason training to get in shape. If I made lateness a crime, my whole team would be left in the parking lot. No one ever shows up at the appointed 6 P.M. time. I'm thrilled when anyone shows up at all.

I hold evening practices three times a week from late June to the start of school in September. On Tuesday, we run on the Marlboro track to work on speed. On Thursday, we run at Holmdel Park to work on hills. On Sunday, we run on the boardwalk in Belmar and beyond to work on distance. I also instruct the boys to run on their own. Ideally, they should train virtually every day in the summer, at least forty miles a week. That's what the best runners do.

In past summers, I've had my whole team at practices. I've also had no one. I've run an entire practice from soup to nuts—warm-up, stretching, striding, speedwork, stretching, striding, cool-down—with one boy. I feel whoever comes deserves to work, no shortcuts.

I'm also in a bind. I can be tougher, demanding, dictatorial. But that will only hurt my efforts. If we lose a couple of key boys from a team of eight, we'll have no chance to excel and achieve the sense of personal heroism I'm trying to instill in the boys. Besides, it's not me. I'm no dictator. I have to use *me*—hard worker, caring fuss-budget, passionate teacher—to get to them. I'm selling myself. Take it or leave it.

The four boys finish their warm-up together and we gather on the track's infield, the football turf, for stretching exercises. They wear long, soccer-style shorts, or cutoffs, anything that approximates what basketball players wear on TV. I tell them authentic, higher-cut running shorts give their legs freer movement and are more comfortable in the heat. They'd rather be dead. They mock my shorts. I mock theirs, saying they're wearing Archie Moore shorts. They look at me blankly.

It's still warm but dry, a perfect night to run. The dropping sun shades the track's backstretch, offering cool reprieve. With the liquid pace of summer taking hold, inner drive must be tapped to negotiate the fast runs to exhaustion we must do to build fitness. The boys know that. Some limber up aggressively, priming their body. Others lazily cut corners or moan. It's part of their act. They finish stretching and complain about their sit-ups. Justin Gallagher can barely get his string-bean body off the ground. He jerks his head forward and calls that a sit-up. I poke fun at Gallagher and he grins. Somewhere in Gallagher's soul is a fierceness that will make him a runner of consequence. I tell him so and he grins a toothy grin. I promise myself I will excavate his fierceness.

Gallagher works long hours in a local banquet hall to save money for a car. That's why he can't make every practice. Michael Dunn's not here tonight. He's working. Other times, kids miss practice because they go to Yankee games, can't get a ride, whatever comes up. You can't enforce passion. One coach told me that I'll feel successful when the boys care about the team as much as I do.

After stretching, we do some hundred-meter strides up the track to get our legs moving and elevate the heart rate, providing a transition into the meat of the workout. Mike Solebello pipes up and says he and Brock won't be at practice for a week because they're going on a fishing trip to Lake Champlain in upstate New York. I tell them they'd better run when they're away. They say they will.

"Where'd you get that extra baggage?" I call to Brock.

He smiles. I know where he got it from. While some of the other guys run spring track, Brock plays baseball. Lot of standing around. Lot of wasted time if you ask me. Brock can run but now he's got to work off some weight. He will. Brock's a mature, systematic athlete whom I made captain as a sophomore. I call him my assistant coach. He can anticipate my instructions beforehand. He volunteers ideas on training. He gets annoyed when teammates horse around.

Brock had not run before St. Rose. That didn't matter. A strong will is a cross-country runner's greatest asset. When Brock and eight other freshmen came out for the team two years ago, I felt I'd struck gold. Dejected by my first frustrating season, I was inspired by these pint-sized kids, who ran like angels, no questions asked, filling my open heart. I taught them everything: how to warm up and subdue side stitches and charge hills and buy running shoes. I met the parents who were warm and trusting and spent six thousand dollars a year so their sons could receive a Catholic school education.

From the outset, the parents buy into my crusade to use running as wellspring of conviction for their sons. They organize car pools, come to cheer at meets, tell me their sons enjoy the team, and in some cases express disbelief when their sons' running ability blossoms. A few parents run themselves; most know nothing about running but sense its value. They are lawyers and laborers and homemakers. They give me free rein with their boys and, if anything, the more discipline, the better for their taste.

Most of the boys had attended parochial grammar schools and I am probably the first Jewish teacher they've known. I sense their surprise that St. Rose would hire a Jewish coach, rare for a Catholic high school. I think their parents are surprised, too, but I try to make them feel at ease with my open-arms style and spiritual consciousness. I may not wear my Jewishness on my sleeve, but I'm totally open about being Jewish. I have deeply Jewish feelings and observe Jewish practice through lifelong teachings at our Reform synagogue, Temple Shaari Emeth. I'm absent from practice on Jewish holy days. The boys know that.

I want to convey to the group that I'm aboveboard on everything, that I will stand up for what's right, and that this quality stems in part from my Jewish background. I want them to know that even though I'm not Catholic I'm on their side—that I'm someone who can be counted to help nurture them, and if I make a mistake it'll be an honest one. I want them to sense that I have a spiritual underpinning, enabling me to understand them at their Catholic core and share in their hopes for the future. We gotta be in this thing together.

But I do have my limits. Last season, Justin Gallagher told me he would have to miss the state finals because of a religious convention in Missouri the same weekend. I said to him, are you kidding? I'd calculated that we needed every man to be a contender. I appealed to Justin's team loyalty, while denying his legitimate need to fulfill a church obligation. I couldn't let go of it. I gently expressed my displeasure to the family, and found support in Justin's father, my comrade Larry, who ultimately said, sorry, but the matter rested in his wife's hands. The good woman prevailed, and that was right. We ran without Justin that time, and still managed to place high in the team standings.

But I can't let that happen this season. I tell Justin straightaway: Be with us all the way to the state finals, or else. He agrees without hesitation. He knows we're a better team and there's more at stake now. The state final in November could be the ultimate triumph for St. Rose. Me and my boys, we can win the big one.

When my aggressive posture surfaces, it stops me in my tracks. I question my motives, my definition of success, whether I'm just another coach who craves a headline and nothing more. I try not to follow the standards of others. I try to make my own Heaven. But too often I feel like a teacher preparing the kids for the final exam. At least then you know the score. As in any educational process, the in-between stuff can be vague and ambiguous. One day Michael Dunn runs his guts out with a smile on his face. The next day he tells me, "Coach, y'know I really don't like running."

I have to be satisfied with imperfection. This is a hard lesson for me, and not the only one by any means. I've learned that parts of me have to change for me to reach these boys and coach effectively. My caring, and my exhaustive knowledge of the sport, are not enough. I have to rid myself of certain presumptions and a disposition that has limited me in relationships and in my own pursuit of athletic achievement. I have to examine how I deal with pain in order to dish out training that will, by necessity, shower the boys with pain. I have to examine how I deal with rejection because you can count on teenage boys blitzing you with some wicked surprises.

Attending Friday-night Shabbat services at our temple helps me weigh my feelings. The prayers, at once mournful and uplifting, have a clarifying effect in delivering the message to "love the good and reject the profane." The rabbi speaks about the interconnect-edness of all things, that "there are no coincidences," and I feel more and more that fate delivered me to St. Rose, that everything I've ever done in my life along with God's sure hand brought me to St. Rose—me, who as a child thought the whole world was Jewish, now working for a Catholic school, trying to do some good for others, and for myself at a time in my life when I surely need it.

Yet when I walk around in my St. Rose cap and my St. Rose sweatshirt, I wonder if I'm committing a sin. God knows, the Catholics have not been friends of the Jews. I read of the growing consensus blaming historic Catholic anti-Semitism for creating a foundation for the Holocaust. But I also read of the pope's pilgrimage to Israel to improve Catholic-Jewish relations and "rediscover the bonds among human beings."

I run with that idea—really the only idea. It's a view hammered from the pulpit by the recently retired rabbi at our temple, Philip Schechter, an inspiring role model. He preaches inclusiveness, works for civil rights, creates an interfaith Thanksgiving service. Rabbi Schechter's posture validates my wish to embrace all peoples, an outlook at odds with what I see in many Jews, who, understandably, seek haven with our own kind. At the start of his career in the turbulent nineteen sixties, Rabbi Schechter was a controversial, muck-raking "hippie rabbi." I wrote passionately about Rabbi Schechter's life in a temple publication upon his retirement. Congregants told me the story brought them to tears. Me, too. Another void.

These boys are a blessing, these Catholic boys, and I feel whole and purposeful as I round them up for evening's test on the track. Ryan, Brock, Justin, and Mike, my feedback for the day, my sustenance. They change from heavy-duty training shoes to lightweight racing flats or spikes for easier strides. Shirts come off, showing taut figures. They seem too small for hearts that must pump furiously to fuel pleading muscles. The boys fidget with their laces, take deep breaths, make small talk.

"Nothing too hard, right, Coach?" says Justin, with a grin that invites a sly comeback.

"Nothing you can't handle," I tell him.

Ryan sprints down the track for final limbering up on his own. Off to the side, Brock and Mike chatter. Usually it's about fishing. They are a pair of straight arrows, hard workers who reinforce a sense of responsibility in each other. No funny business. Mike's a little edgy, and it shows on his face. A sprinter on the spring track squad, Mike's committed to acquiring the stamina for cross-country. He knows we need him. And I keep telling Mike that cross-country will build his strength for track, where his specialty is the 400 meters. I remind him that Michael Johnson, the world record holder and Olympic champion in the 400, runs cross-country. Well, I think he does. I use any leverage I can think of for motivation. Whatever the boys believe works.

Training boys for cross-country competition, in which most races are 5 kilometers, or 3 miles 188 yards, and the terrain is on hilly park trails, is a test for me as well. The canvas of running options is endless. Distance, speed, fast, slow, hard, easy, track, turf, hills, road. The concepts present themselves like an array of paints to be selected, one palette today, another tomorrow. There is no foolproof method for success, and that's what makes success so sweet. You create your own path to mastery.

But you do need a system; the running cannot be done haphazardly. The boys like a system, too. They are experienced enough to understand the building blocks, the elements that strengthen you. It may not prevent them from skipping practice for a Yankee game, but when they run with me they can feel secure that I've got a plan. It's written down in my thick spiral notebook marked *Training Log*, which I clutch as I spell out the workout for the boys, who line up on the starting line.

"Repeat thousands," I announce. "Five of them, with a six hundred rest in between." I remind them about even pacing, being able to complete the workout, finishing strong. The boys are mostly concerned about times, asking how fast should we run, Coach? Good question. It's the first workout and everyone's at a different level. Ryan and Mike are coming off the track season and should be pretty fit. Justin played lacrosse and got in some running. Brock did a lot of nothing in baseball. It's all too messy and incoherent for my taste. This is not a group capable of running together, as a team, right now. I tell Ryan, the fittest, to go out at a slowish 85 seconds a lap, everyone else tuck in behind, and see how that feels. Agreed.

I blow my gold-plated whistle, a team gift, and they're off. Too fast, of course. "Slow, slow," I urge. They ease up. Ryan sets the pace, holding back, as easy for him as for a jaguar. Mike's second, then Justin, then Brock with a ballplayer's tush weighing him down. They pass me single file after a 400-meter lap. "Eighty-five. Perfect." On the backstretch, I shout encouragement, calling their names. "C'mon, Mike, work at it." I watch them closely, checking their shoulders, arms, knee lift, looking for any flaw to correct. "Elbows in, Justin, elbows in." Justin cranks his elbows closer to his body, enabling his arms to flow up and back—better than side to side which wastes energy.

I need every edge, inch, second, nanosecond. My small team, and the intricacies of cross-country scoring, demand it. In a meet, the places of a team's first five runners across the finish are added up, and low score wins. You're allowed to run a maximum of seven runners; your sixth and seventh runners also "count," as their placings can push back scoring runners from opposing teams. A team's seventh and last runner can finish, say, 50th in a field of 150 runners and still play a crucial role in determining the outcome.

This team dynamic endows cross-country with a humanity that no other sport can claim. The top five runners are all of equal importance; the sixth and seventh, the understudies, are close. This makes cross-country open, free, available, the most egalitarian pursuit. You show up, try hard. You matter. You can't beat that. There are no tryouts, no boundaries, no cuts, no shortcuts.

Tonight's running, like all running, says so. Ryan covers the first 1,000-meter repetition, two and a half laps, in 3:29, right on target. Mike is two strides back in 3:31 with Justin in his shadow in 3:32 and Brock lagging badly in 3:40. It's a leap of faith for me to imagine Brock lean and sharp and pressing Ryan for the top position on our squad come fall, but Brock's come through before. Two years ago, when these guys were top-notch freshmen—the "Fabulous Freshmen," I called them—Brock taught everyone a lesson money can't buy.

In the first meet of the season, at the St. Dominic's Invitational in Jersey City, we tied Morristown High for first place in the freshman race. To break the tie, officials used the sixth-runner rule. Brock, running the first race of his life, was our sixth man that day. He finished ahead of the sixth runner from Morristown, and St. Rose won. Brock, who had placed thirteenth more than a minute behind our first runner, Ryan, was the hero. Had Brock—or anyone on our team, for that matter—run a few seconds slower, we would have lost.

Now, in early summer, as the sun sets and my boys run their laps, that's what possesses me: seconds. That's what this season will come down to: seconds. Each boy must improve, must shave seconds and run faster than before, even by a full minute because that's what I tell them over and over: Everyone must run a minute faster than last year, it can be done, I've seen it done, all you have to do is train hard over the summer. Put in the miles, build a base, a foundation, gain the strength to sustain months of running and handle the fierce combat of fall competition.

That's why we're doing 1,000s tonight. Strength. I'm asking the boys not for blazing speed but to hold a firm, steady pace, take a short rest, then do it again. The total of the five 1,000s adds up to our race distance of 5,000 meters. I will use this framework for the entire season, playing with the required time for each 1,000 and the rest "interval" between each one. In subsequent workouts, the times will get faster and the rest shorter so that the workout, when stitched together, is ultimately as demanding as a race.

At least that's the plan. After jogging a 600 in about four minutes, the boys are ready again. I whistle them onward. Ryan leads this one in 3:23, Mike shows smart pacing with another 3:31, Justin loses ground and contorts his face, frozen in the struggle, until he finds relief past the finish. Brock's even farther back and wears the hard, knowing look of resignation. This is a good slap in the face for Brock, and he doesn't mind hearing that from me. He's done enough for tonight. I instruct him to switch gears and finish up with an easy mile. Justin will tough it out. His father insists on it. I go along with that. Can't forget about the kid's fierceness.

The pace is sedate for Ryan, who seems too sharp for his own good. Easy, boy, you want to be at your best—*peaking* is the operative word—in November. Ryan clicks off 80 seconds a lap for 3:18, and 3:18 again, while Mike wavers slightly in 3:33 and 3:37, good for the sprinter, and Justin grimaces from behind. I don't mind

Ryan running faster, but what's best for the boys is steady progress week by week. Each time, we need to leave room for improvement. It's a long season. Ryan can't hold the pace in his last 1,000, finishing in 3:30, the original goal. Mike, doubled over after his fourth repetition, needs extra rest to sustain the set of five. I give him another sixty seconds. He's thankful and comes home with the crease of a smile in 3:39.

This is the hardest training we know: long intervals. *Long* meaning two or more hard laps around the track, *interval* the catchall term for repeating the hard runs on fairly short rest. Short intervals like repeat one-lappers are no piece of cake, either, but tonight's 1,000s will assuredly raise the boys' heart rates to maximum level and they will feel that cold, relentless assault that forces you to decide if you can take it or will give up. Not giving up is what cross-country success boils down to. The fitter you are, the less often that option has to come up.

Giving up, letting the competitor in your gaze get away like a vessel on the horizon, reveals a submissive, immature reaction to pain. Running hard tests the body like little else. What teenage boy, with today's comforts, knows such stark physical suffering? The only vocabulary he has in response is surrender. I must create a new, spiritual vocabulary, a new thought pattern and a new realm; really, a new existence, one that becomes familiar and even welcome as a path toward righteousness. After all, noble suffering is a Christian doctrine. My boys will have to accept it from a Jewish voice.

I must try to eliminate the option entirely. Giving up can't be a choice at St. Rose. It's not an option at Christian Brothers Academy, where marine-like enforcement quells any weakness. But my soft sell might be too soft. I can't sell recognition. Cross-country is back-of-the-bus compared to basketball and football, which gets a seventy-page stand-alone season preview in the local paper. We get the agate.

I know how to sell hard work. I've worked hard since my teens, starting by helping my father in the summers with his soft-drink business, schlepping heavy cases of bottled soda to bodegas in Brooklyn's worst neighborhoods. I've always used hard work to compensate for a lack of skill or knowledge. I don't learn that fast but I try hard. I think that's okay for my boys, too.

But I don't know if I can teach guts because I'm not sure I've ever had any. I never spoiled for a fight, have little tolerance for confrontation, and gave up routinely when I ran in high school myself. This is new territory for me, but maybe I'm already learning because it probably takes some guts to coach a high school boys' cross-country team—to look boys in the eye and reveal yourself to them while asking them to do the same.

After running, the boys lean forward in exhaustion, bracing themselves with hands on knees. "Let's get our shirts on, or you'll get chilled," I insist. "C'mon, shirts on." They slug water, make a circle, and stretch. I assess the workout, saying it was a decent first day but we have our work cut out for us. I deliver my mantra: Come to team practices, run on your own, do the right thing, and inner satisfaction, the best reward, will follow.

It's getting dark and parents are waiting in the parking lot with their motors running. I hustle the boys away with one last urgency: "Tell the other guys to show up, will ya?"

My boys pay me no mind. Instead, they buzz about the Yankees and catching trout.

2

Running Rebels

"Okay, who ran while I was away?"

It's midsummer at Holmdel Park, which feels primitive and newly discovered in July. The fields, swarming with runners and parents in starched shirts and cameras flying from their shoulders come fall, are barren except for a dog chasing a Frisbee. Few teams are in training yet. Occasionally we see a squad from South Jersey pile out of a bus for a look-see at the course, which will host the state championships in November.

I wait for a response, but the St. Rose faces look away. "Lavender?" I know Lavender ran but he doesn't want to seem like a goody two-shoes by speaking up. "I was out there, Coach," he finally says with thinly parted lips. Otherwise, silence.

I'm back from twelve days covering the Olympic Track and Field Trials in Sacramento, California. I'd told the boys how to train while I was away, but for most it's too easy to cheat when the teacher's not looking. Running when the coach isn't even in town? That takes discipline, but without discipline you may as well pack it in. You're no cross-country runner.

The boys straggle in, most after the 6 P.M. start. They arrive wearing Yankee shirts, Bermuda shorts, and mischievous grins. From out of the blue, Gallagher says, "Coach, can I run the New York City Marathon?" Gallagher loves to invite my jibes. I laugh hard. "Sure you can," I say with a gently mocking tone.

John Leschak, the sophomore, invites jibes without saying a word. He's hardly Catholic school material with spiked hair, thick chains around his neck, studded bracelets, and colorful shorts down to his knees. While not the soldier-straight cross-country runner, John is a gifted artist who creates posters for the team and has a perpetual smile that says, *What, me worry?* Leschak trains as hard as anyone. But I don't think a bohemian like him will last long at St. Rose.

I probe further into the boys' recent running and just then we see the Mater Dei team, fifteen-strong, assemble across the meadow. Perfect timing. Mater Dei is the defending state champion in our Parochial B division, as well as winner of our dual-meet conference. I deliver my stump speech: Mater Dei is our chief rival, their whole squad comes to every practice, they're working hard with team unity, what's wrong with us?

Mike Solebello offers that he ran a few times but not that much, not every day, how can you expect him to run every day, he's working with his father's construction crew, but he did follow the coach's dictates, maybe not to the letter, but he did cooperate, he did stretch before and after running, maybe not every single stretching exercise but most of them, and he's not to be lumped with anyone who totally screws up and doesn't give a shit.

And I respect that. Solebello's a fine boy. If I had a son, I would want a Solebello. He has strong sense of right and wrong, and if I can tilt that strength toward conviction, I'm home. I know I can count on his mother, Sue, a runner herself. She greets with me with a delicious smile and is so pleased that the team has given Mike good grounding. Still, at one point, his grades suffer, prompting Sue to call me and say, "Can you speak to Mike? He looks up to you."

Every so often, I receive a small bouquet like that—a real biggie, who am I kidding?—that makes me feel warm and teary and reminds me that all this coaching has made me long a little less for my daughters since they left home. I don't know if that's good or bad. I still miss them terribly, need them like a man in the desert needs drink, but working with the boys helps balance me, providing a well to deposit my passion and caring.

With each bit of evidence that I'm doing some good, I feel closer to my faith, fulfilling the Jewish commandment to do *mitzvot*, to help someone in need, especially the young. Each act, like patting a boy on the back or telling his mother what a sweet kid he is, renews me as though tasting holy water. At that moment when one of my boys feels ten feet tall, everything else seems to recede, and it is him and me, hand to hand, inching closer to the view espoused by the theologian Aquinas: "Grace builds on nature." I find I need that essence daily.

In California, despite the busy schedule, I feel empty after a few days. Long track trips, even to Athens or Seville, no longer excite me as they once did. I miss home, miss my wife, call her often. I try to get into strict routines and work hard doing interviews and chasing down stories. Inevitably, loneliness consumes me and I eat and drink too much. I feel out of sync with colleagues, many of them single or divorced, who seem happy to be away.

I find that, after all these years, the competition itself rarely stirs me, certainly not compared with the fervor I feel when my boys race. At the trials, I have the urge to check on the team but don't want to seem overbearing. Fortunately, I have an excuse. An article I'd written for *The New York Times* on running the mile comes out, and who turns up in the big photo used to illustrate the piece: Ryan Lavender.

A few weeks before, I'd entered the mile at a local all-comers meet for a "Weekend Warrior" story in the *Times* entertainment section. Though I run regularly, I rarely race anymore, but for purposes of a story I will gladly abuse my body. When I happen to mention the meet to the team, Lavender, who cannot pass up a race, says he's also planning to run the all-comers meet, in the mile. Me against Lavender? I hope my presence doesn't spook him out. It doesn't. Lavender winds up winning with panache. I place sixth, almost a lap behind, in considerable pain. But I get my story.

It's a good thing I'm there, too. In addition to the mile, Lavender tells me he's going to do the long jump. Cross-country runners do not long jump. Their bodies are better suited to calf roping. But that's Lavender, the try-anything kid. Even though he's hungry for success, he likes to affect the aura that running's not so important that he can't fool around, risking injury, in the long jump or hurdles. In this regard, there's a touch of the British aristocracy in him. Sport should not be taken too seriously, but dammit, you'd better win.

While that exit strategy might be of some value to an Olympic athlete looking for reprieve, it's dangerous for a high school runner. It offers an easy out, a ready excuse, a way to avoid not only failure but also success. You never commit. You shrink from your potential. In Lavender's case, I think he feels that if he does excel, and makes a name for himself state-wide, he'll have to try that much harder to defend his turf. And he doesn't know if he's up to the task. As the playwright Arthur Miller said in one interview, "Success is the great man-eater. Surviving it is as hard as attaining it, if not harder."

Lavender projects confidence, and will run the state-meet course fast on his own when it doesn't count. But inside, Lavender churns with doubt.

Naturally, I want to help him sort this out. Right now, I'm not sure how. I can tell from his weak eyes, his occasional mournful gaze, his reticence, that he feels isolated by his parents' divorce. Karen and Dennis Lavender are good people who want the best for Ryan. But evidently their rancor has continued since their split and Ryan is often in the middle of it. One week I hear Ryan is living with his dad; the next week, he is bickering with his dad and moving in with Mom. Careful not to take sides, I speak with both parents, who admit their helplessness in guiding their son.

It would be convenient to consider Ryan's reckless bent, like his long jump predilection, as a cry for help. Hurt yourself, that'll get Mom-and-Dad's attention, maybe even draw them together for once. It's hard for me to know what to make of this situation. All I know is, I've got a kid on my team with the stride of an angel who thinks he's going to long jump.

To prevent Lavender from busting up his knees and ruining the whole season—for him, the team, the school, God, and of course me—in a freakin' stupid all-comers meet, I collect myself after our mile race and discreetly grab Lavender around the shoulders and walk him off the track to a wooded spot behind the grandstand where I took a desperate piss moments before.

"Ryan, make the old coach happy. And do yourself a favor. Don't do the long jump. Humor me." He agrees, but just so I won't totally cramp his style, Ryan decides to run the 100-meter sprint. You can only tear your hamstring muscle doing that.

Even though my *Times* story is about guys my age trying to

develop speed for the mile, the editors choose a picture of the teenage Lavender, whom I barely mention in the story. Go figure. But I'm thrilled to see Ryan's ego stroked, and sure enough, when I phone his home from California, his father tells me they've gotten congratulatory calls from all over the country. Hey, I say, it's just the coach taking care of his own.

I never imagined I'd have teenage boys to care for when I walked into St. Rose for the first time four years ago. After sending out my résumé, I was called in for an interview by the athletic director at the time, Michael Robertson. I'd barely heard of St. Rose, and when I walked the halls and saw pictures of Jesus Christ everywhere and inhaled the church-like smell of the place, I told myself, fine, meet the guy, but they're just not hiring a Jew. For all I knew, Catholic schools still taught that the Jews killed Christ.

I took an immediate liking to Robertson, who'd seen my *Times* articles and was at least confident that I knew running. He didn't know if I could really coach. Neither did I.

The interview went fine and I waited for the "Jewish" question. It had to come up. One of us had to say something. Finally, Robertson said, "Don't take this the wrong way. We don't care if you're Jewish. But what about you—will you feel comfortable in a Catholic school environment?"

Fair question. The answer was yes and no. I only told Mike the *yes* part, that I cut my teeth covering Catholic high school track in the sixties, that running had an Irish Catholic tradition I'd been immersed in, and that I was quite at ease in a Catholic environment—or any environment for that matter, just gimme a team to coach. The *no* part was that as a Jew I felt somewhat disloyal with the idea of "serving" the cross, if that's what I would be doing as I tried to nurture St. Rose student-athletes.

Robertson hired me. My salary would be fifteen hundred dollars for the season, which I calculated was less than minimum wage. No matter. I would have coached for nothing.

Before the position could be official, I had to sign off on the school's Christian Witness Statement, required of all faculty, to celebrate Christ, promote Christian values, and live a Christian lifestyle. I signed it, focusing on the command to be a "person of prayer," one with a "deep faith." That I felt I was. In my mind, I separated Catholic from coaching. I didn't realize then that I would be able to fuse them effectively as one.

After the frustrations of my first season in '97, when the naughty-boy seniors ruled the roost, I was presented with a gift the next summer: nine eager and innocent freshmen, some with running experience from grammar school. Impressionable boys who wanted to run! Thank you, God. The boys got new training shoes just as I instructed them, came to practice, were gleeful with each bit of success. I ran alongside the slower boys to nurse them along. Parents marveled at their gains. So did I.

We all learned together. The boys, too raw to understand training concepts, mostly learned they could trust me. If I told them how they would feel doing a workout, how they would gain from it, and everything transpired as I'd said, the boys could allow their running to take root without resistance. Mainly I used trial and error to see how much I could push them. If anything, I erred on the side of less, giving the boys a few miles at a time to keep their legs fresh and ensure long-term development.

I enjoyed the boys' company and thrilled at their progress. They were skin and bones, all limbs, sweet and purposeful. They would act goofy like fourteen-year-olds should and they needed their space, literally. Boys cannot stand still and must have room to be physical and horse around. The St. Rose girls would practice when we did and I would marvel at their decorum and obedience. We boys were a ragtag bunch from the get-go.

But we could run. When the season got under way, St. Rose won the freshman division at almost every meet we entered and loomed as one of the state's brightest young teams. We got written up in the *Newark Star-Ledger*. Each victory rallied the team that much more and, as for me, I was on cloud nine all fall. I could see how the coaches I'd admired produced great teams. More than in any other sport, in cross-country what you put in (coaches included) is what you get out.

Lavender was the freshman star, collecting individual titles even though he'd shoot out too fast. I was careful not to treat him any differently. He'd also been the champion of the grammar school ranks and I didn't want anyone to think we had a prima donna on our hands. I was proud when his father told me he'd chosen St. Rose over nationally ranked Christian Brothers Academy because he'd heard good things about me and didn't care for the CBA coach's stern style. But was that Dad's way of telling me I'd better produce? No, Dennis Lavender just wanted the right fit for Ryan.

Ryan seemed to need his victories more than relish them. I spent the whole season trying to get him to pace himself better. Start easy and come on strong, that was the message and also the most fun. The boy had talent and could win despite any tactical flaw. As luck would have it, I missed Ryan's biggest win, our team's biggest win, in the Shore Conference Championship. On the day of the meet, which draws forty-five schools from Monmouth and Ocean Counties, St. Rose went up against mighty CBA in the freshman race. Ryan took first and our team soundly defeated CBA.

I had to wait on pins and needles for the results while out on

Long Island at a nephew's Bar Mitzvah. When I'd told the boys I couldn't go to the meet, they did not question the reason. A few had been to Bar Mitzvahs and commented on the amount of food and theatrical, theme parties. We shared a fascination with the need for such excess.

The St. Rose girls' coach, Bill Jasko, a buddy of mine who teaches at the school, looked after the squad. He was amazed himself as he read me the results. Nobody beats CBA. And we did it without a key runner, who was sidelined with shin splints. I figured then that if our Lavender-led freshmen could outrun CBA, it stood to reason that this same group years later as juniors and seniors could at least match the Colts in the big varsity invitational events. I had a lot to learn.

On some summer nights, CBA turns up at Holmdel Park. When they congregate, twenty-five or thirty serious boys in military precision, I try and get my boys to avert their eyes so they won't feel outdone. It reminds me of the Bill Murray movie *Meatballs*, in which one elite summer camp has computer classes, fancy trips, and Henry Kissinger as a guest speaker. That's CBA. It's an all-boys academy with an enrollment of twelve hundred on broad, manicured grounds like a miniature Princeton. The school has indoor and outdoor tracks, and lush park trails at its doorstep. It has a coach, Tom Heath, who runs a rigorous, year-round, take-no-prisoners program. CBA has tradition: Each new squad inherits toughness and pride.

St. Rose has nothing. No track, no school grounds, no running tradition. We have a parking lot. Our athletic fields, including a murky cross-country course, are ten miles away abutting an airport. When school begins, CBA identifies the good freshman runners and directs them to the cross-country team. At St. Rose, I attend a freshman orientation, promise kids the world, and mostly get comments from Johnny like, "Yeah, I ran in grammar school but I'm going out for soccer."

This is frustrating but I don't let it deter me. In front of my boys, I never defer to CBA or any team. We can be as good, I tell them. The CBA guys are not born runners. They're just like you with one difference: They try harder. I have to convince myself of that first.

We have come to Holmdel Park this evening to run hills, find shaded trails, and commit the race course to memory. We must learn every twist and turn, up and down, where to hold pace, where to surge. Holmdel has more hills than most courses, including the feared "Bowl," a long, steep pitch midway that can whip you silly. The Bowl is omnipotent. It dictates strategy and requires unwavering strength built over the summer.

Today we're skipping the Bowl. I use lesser hills as a prelude. I don't want to risk burning the kids out. Our small team cannot afford to lose one runner. We'll get to the Bowl soon enough. And since it looks like the boys have been doing little training on their own, they're not ready to tackle the Bowl. They need more seasoning.

But we cannot avoid the heat. Even at night it's sweltering and I make sure the boys drink plenty of water. I collect everyone—Lavender, Solebello, Gallagher, Dunn, Silvestri, Leschak and my senior Chris Ruhl—and send them on five laps of what I call the "Woods Loop." Each lap, part uphill and part downhill, is a little over a mile. It's mostly shaded but in the humidity the boys sweat badly, and as they pass me after each loop I spray them generously with a water bottle. Some boys duck, others approach me for a hit like panting dogs.

I track the boys' lap times so I can anticipate their arrival and urge them on to the next loop. I shout pointers on taking the hills: knees up, body erect, gaze straight ahead. "Lean in from the hips," I repeat. "The hips." Tired runners tend to sag, their torsos listing. "The hips," I call again and again. "Work the arms. Work the arms."

The boys listen, bolting into proper position as they hear my voice. They want to do well, succeed, achieve their best. At a place like CBA, that effort is not so much enforced as molded by an environment, a veritable community, that treasures running as a sport and attitude. The runners with promise are chosen for special assignment, the cross-country team, and soccer be damned.

Tonight's group of seven might well be my entire team. I've lost many of the school's best runners to soccer, which has run amok nationwide and become cross-country's Public Enemy Number One. Most cross-country teams have upward of twenty athletes. You can barely sustain a program with less than a dozen. The outstanding distance runner at St. Rose, a boy who's won two state titles in the 3,200 meters in spring track, plays soccer in the fall even though he's an average player. When I appeal to his father, saying the boy can earn a college scholarship with his cross-country running, Dad's answer is that his son "has been playing soccer since he was seven." I want to punch someone.

I have no problem with the game of soccer, which is terrific. Both my daughters played and gained from soccer, and many very fine runners start out as soccer players. But as my kids' experiences ran their course in the mid-eighties, soccer started to become the national youth suburban status symbol it is today. Now community programs grab kids like cults. They have them compete as pipsqueaks for traveling-team berths, take them to costly, faraway tournaments, and disdain other sports, and other aspects of life, that may get in the way of coaches' fantasies or compromise the unbridled power of league officials. At our synagogue, the rabbi has to field complaints from parents that their little darlings cannot fulfill a religious school obligation because of a soccer date.

And that's not the half of it. A high school cross-country coach in Castro Valley, California, let loose on the web about girls on his team trying to play club soccer as well as run in the fall because their soccer coaches demanded participation twelve months a year. The cross-country coach said his runners would tell him they couldn't run in a meet because of a soccer match the same day. Finally, the coach put his foot down and told his girls they'd have to make a choice: soccer or cross-country, but not both. The coach called soccer—again, not the game, but the ethic—"a poison."

I don't know if I'd go that far. But soccer-driven parental excess and the idea that "my child can do no wrong" have gotten so bad that abrasive behavior of soccer moms and dads on the sidelines has escalated to abuse of referees, use of foul language, confrontation with opposing-team parents and even fistfights with coaches. Lovely example for the kids. This headline-making trend has rightfully caused alarm among educators, and the entrenched soccer community has begrudgingly gotten the message. In a number of cities, mandatory classes have been set up to teach soccer parents (not their children) how to behave at games.

Cross-country parents, on the other hand, are courteous and respectful on the sidelines. They wait patiently for the runners to pass and console their exhausted sons and daughters at the finish. They applaud the opposition as well. It's the effort that is cherished. The rigors of cross-country foster a heartfelt grandeur, yielding a sweetness and generosity too easily crushed in other sports dependent on mass approval or professional prima donnas.

These differences reflect on national values gone haywire and get to the heart of what consumes me as I work with my boys. Nothing riles me more than parents who shower their kids with possessions of privilege and never say no. Whether the gift is fancy clothes or a guaranteed spot in the starting lineup, the result is the same. Children learn that superficial ownership, a sense of entitlement, and the easy way out are what life is all about. I know, it's an old story. That's the worst part. Kids are more and more indulged, our entire culture sways to the rhythms of a twelve-year-old's buying power and taste, and no one seems to care. We accept it.

In America, we have created a mass, uniform Hollywood culture that captures young people before they have a chance to develop their own good ideas. *This* is the poison. It seems to have anesthetized kids into following a gargantuan celebrity-seeking pack, impairing their physical health, stunting emotional growth, creating spiritual ennui—and driving cross-country coaches like me nuts.

With running as the linchpin, I want to convince my boys to reject the ornamental culture, as one social critic put it, and come over to the other side, the holy side if you will. Only then can they truly dedicate themselves to fulfilling their potential and traveling the path to good citizenship. To some extent, the Running Roses are already on the other side, or at least on the fence. They attend Catholic school. They are taught Christian values. I know; I read the mission statement.

I'm no proselytizer, but I see this as a matter of nonconformity. Getting teenagers to cross boundaries may be harder than running the Bowl. But I want to wed those two ideas into one beautiful, soaring ethic: that acquiring the ability to conquer the Bowl in competition is emblematic of going your own way. I should have plenty of ammunition at my disposal. Jesus, after all, was the ultimate rebel with a cause.

The boys run past me for the final tour of the Woods Loop. Ryan and Brock come first, setting the pace. Ryan's stride is classically long, like a champion miler's. His feet snap off the turf. Brock, his baseball behind leaner now, has a steady, powerful gait. He puts his shoulders into his running, making up for lack of quickness. They don't speak, or at least I don't hear them. I want them to talk. I want Ryan and Brock to be close. I want them to be friendly rivals, spurring each other on.

Close behind, in a threesome, are Justin, Mike Dunn and Mike Solebello. When he tires, Justin contorts his face like someone standing in front of those funny mirrors at a carnival. His neck cords like a road map. I tell him to relax his face, but he insists on fashioning a frightening countenance. Dunn, self-consciously small, is growing in height if not in effort. He should be up with Ryan and Brock but he dogs it, almost arrogantly so, as though to say, *Sorry, Coach, you can shout all you want, I'm just not running that hard.* On the other hand, Solebello, the converted sprinter, won't relent. What self-respecting construction worker would?

Trailing are Leschak, his chains jangling incongruently in the bucolic trails, and Ruhl, in his fourth year of cross-country. When Ruhl started with me, I had a large contingent of freshmen, but he's the only one left—he and Sgt. Pepper, I hope. "Jeez, Lennon," I mutter whenever I think of him. From that original group, I lost boys to other teams, to doing nothing, to disciplinary measures. One boy bullied a weaker kid, at about the same time bullying was implicated in fatal school shootings. Fed up, I notified the bully's parents that I was going to drop him. The boy quit before I could.

After forty minutes, the boys complete the workout and cool out. I spray them once more as they stretch and chat. They all get along but they're not one seamless social group. I would like that, too. I want them to care about each other so they will feel shame if they miss practice or give up in a race. I wonder if I hope for too much.

I also ask myself if the boys are too soft. At sixteen or seventeen, are they incapable of absorbing the "punishment" necessary to excel? The former mile star Marty Liquori has said that affluence spoils runners and the needier, the better at the championship level. That's probably true for most sports but especially so in distance running. To endure the grind of running, to pile on thousands of miles, to keep going when your body pleads for mercy or you're simply not in the mood—this perseverance is not very well sustained by someone who's got Daddy's business to fall into. A life of hardship is one reason Kenyans and Ethiopians dominate Olympic distance running. Running can be the ticket to a better life.

I drum that notion into my boys. Fortunately, I can count on their families for support. The St. Rose parents do not appear to baby their kids as I see other parents do. The boys don't get everything handed to them. Ryan Lavender's father, a lawyer, is a partner in a school for the disabled, and Ryan often works there to help out. The guys all have jobs, saving for cars or college. But they are still part of a culture that promotes immediate gratification. The slam dunk rules.

To run to the ultimate, as I want these boys to do, is to be in touch with a deep need, or at least an acceptance, of bettering yourself through suffering. It's a good suffering. It's a religious idea of suffering. It's a suffering not only for personal growth but also for the greater good. There are souls to be saved. Ask those at Columbine High.

There are times when running hurts so much it consumes you—like when you pound up the Bowl jelly-legged in a race—but it's a temporary suffering. I tell the boys that the suffering is a test.

The pain passes. Get through the suffering and you enter a different world, a pristine world, where you have a higher consciousness, an exquisite understanding of life, a taste of hardship, and hardship conquered. Then the running is smoother and more powerful than you ever imagined.

I don't use these exact words, but this is my message.

It's a lot to ask, but what are we doing as teachers if we don't insist that kids strive to reach the next level? The great Australian running coach Percy Cerutty told his teenage protégé Herb Elliott, who would become the 1960 Olympic 1500-meter champion, "Pain is the purifier. Embrace it."

I want my boys to feel running's purifying effect. I don't know if the CBA boys feel it, but they surely run like they do. St. Rose can be a great, seamless team like CBA, I know we can. When the boys finish a hard workout in the Holmdel hills, as they did today, I study their faces, looking for signals. I see contented faces. I see creases of smiles. The boys are spent but satisfied. We're on our way.

World cross-country champion Lynn Jennings once told me she feels cleansed after a hard run, and that's how the boys look now: cleansed. Between gulps of water, Solebello says, "Coach, what do you think, are we in good shape?" No one ever asks me that but Solebello. He knows the answer but needs to hear me say it. It's refreshing to see a boy open with his needs. I give a stock assessment, saying so far, so good, but we have a lot more work to do. Solebello gulps more water. The other boys say nothing.

Every season begins in June when I hold my summer training orientation. I gather the team in the St. Rose gym to review our plans and try to motivate the boys. I display our trophies, show a running film, serve cookies. I tell stories about great runners, especially those from New Jersey, but afterward the meeting always seems flat. I don't notice a lot of can't-wait-to-run excitement. Maybe that's just boys.

This year, with their third season of cross-country ahead of them, I felt the boys were ready for some thought-provoking pearls. I pulled out a brilliant quote from *The Loneliness of the Long-Distance Runner*, in which the rebellious young protagonist, Colin Smith, says: "I couldn't see anybody, and I knew what the loneliness of the long-distance runner running across the country felt like, realizing that as far as I was concerned this feeling was the only honesty and realness in the world, and I knowing it would be no different ever, no matter what I felt at odd times, and no matter what anybody else tried to tell me."

That's us, rebels, I told the team proudly. Nobody spoke until Gallagher chirped, "Coach, are we gonna have the cookies soon because I have to go . . ."

I can take that. I taught school for nine years, didn't I? I think I read the *Loneliness* quote as much for myself as for the boys. Smith's words could be mine. In the film based on the Alan Sillitoe work, Tom Courtenay plays Smith, who snubs convention, sees through adult hypocrisy, and uses cross-country running as a weapon.

While religious practice is thought of as a natural mainstream act, I see Judaism as a form of rebellion. Differentness affords rebellion. But while wisecracking Seinfeldian Judaism has melded into the mainstream, the Jewish mandate to pray, learn, and serve others is still way out there, gushing rebellion as when Jews stand up for the poor, the abused, the downtrodden. I find comfort in the rebel posture and at every after-school practice, when I gather with my boys and try to teach them the right thing, I feel like we're in a secret huddle, and screw the idiots who don't get it.

Cross-country and rebellion are natural allies. Running across the meadow or through the woods while the rest of America sleeps strikes me as a defiant, liberating act. Cross-country originated as a gentlemanly endeavor in England in the eighteen sixties to keep rowers in shape during the winter. It spread to other nations, including the United States, where it became a high school and college sport at the turn of the century. A 1907 *New York Times* story aptly characterized cross-country by stating: "One of its greatest attractions lies in the fact that it is absolutely free. There is no possibility of gain connected from it." No gate receipts, the *Times* said. No professionalism.

While professional sports grew and corruption followed, cross-country remained purely amateur, the lowest link on the sports food chain when I ran in high school in the early sixties. Growing up, I was known for two things among my friends: a knack for running, and a fiercely guarded independence.

My independence, no less cemented today, is rooted in my Judaism. As a child in the orthodox Boro Park section of Brooklyn, I succumbed to the strict practices of my parents, who kept kosher and forbade riding, buying a newspaper, or even answering the phone on the Sabbath. Even though as I got older I had gentile friends and helped them toss tinsel onto their Christmas trees, I thrilled to be the rabbi of our synagogue's junior congregation and felt an overpowering awe when attending services with my grandparents—at a walk-up shul smelling of haggard men, or in a majestic temple where the rabbis marched like popes.

I was shaped by the idea that a superior goodness and Judaism were uniquely one, and that marshaling the discipline to lead a righteous life was as important as life itself. No one dared speak in the open of that terrible event that had happened in Europe, but the barbed-wire picture of emaciated bodies occasionally seen was a potent reminder that being Jewish—and Jewishly Jewish—was a lifelong commandment beyond question.

When my family moved to the more contemporary Sheepshead Bay section of Brooklyn, I was tested daily. None of my close Jewish friends attended Hebrew school or did anything Jewish. I was known not only for outrunning everyone in schoolyard play but also for refusing to eat pizza or anything not kosher. I finally broke down around age sixteen.

In high school, like some of my St. Rose boys, I ran cross-country mainly to get in shape for track. I fancied myself a sprinter, and track was cool. A world record in the 100-yard dash made headlines. Before the seventies running boom gave distance running some cachet, cross-country runners were thought of as skinny nerds with no athletic talent. That was not far from the truth.

In 1963-64, my senior year, an American, Buddy Edelen, set a world record for the marathon with a handkerchief tied around his head, standard-issue protection against the sun. As Frank Shorter would admit with pride, distance runners were strange birds. Shorter, whose cross-country titles would lead to his Olympic marathon victory in 1972, ran early wearing a ponytail. It was not the fashion statement of today's ultra-hip Silicon Valley male but the straggly hippie statement of a man who disdained authority and lived in a shack in order to run.

Even though running turned professional and people like Shorter deservedly made out well, cross-country at its heart is still kids running through the woods to exhaustion on a Saturday morning. To me, the sport embodies honor and dignity, and at meets I am often moved to tears by how much kids will put out, collapsing into adult arms or falling splat on the ground at the finish.

You can't buy that courage. I consider my team's progress a moral compass, a way to see the effects of passionate teaching on young minds. For every up, however, there's a downer. One day the boys run like deer, another day they lag and balk and their legs and arms don't seem to go together. Whey they sag, I sag. I find myself dependent on the boys' energy level and attitude.

I know I can count on Lennon to pick me up, and when he finally shows at Holmdel Park later in summer as the heat recedes, he talks big, sweet-mouths any girl within earshot, and disses any boy not up to his standard of cool. Sgt. Pepper's back! Mr. Personality. You can't help but love this guy. His wide smile and twinkling eyes take over the park, and any talk of running among team members is replaced by girls and parties and the social scene at the beach. I overhear a lot of sexual boasting and it's hard for me to believe that these sweet, tentative boys—Lennon excluded, of course—have ever touched a girl.

Lennon has a way of taking over the coaching, too, directing the stretching exercises, the sit-ups, or the jogging the boys do to warm up. He's too charming to argue with, and to be honest I don't mind having a senior assert himself as a team leader. But what kind of influence will Lennon be? His incessant joking finally ticks me off, but I'll give him plenty of space as long as he puts oomph into his running.

"So how much running have you been doing?" I ask him.

"Plenty, Coach, plenty." Uh-huh.

Lennon, a basketball star at St. Rose, says he's been playing in a summer league. He feigns taking a shot, jumping with his arm skyward and hand tipping as though releasing a ball. Few of the boys are pure runners. Ruhl and Silvestri still play baseball, and I fret over possible leg injuries from sliding into bases.

My one possible freshman so far, Anthony Arnold, plays soccer, and his mother says he's still not sure which sport he'll choose.

Arnold's a wiry boy who can run. I practically beg the mother to see the light, but she defers to her son. One night she calls and says Anthony is going to try out for soccer team but if that doesn't work out he'll consider cross-country.

"Good luck," I tell her. To myself, I say, *Oh, fuck it.*

Lennon can't stop talking. He's on stage even when he runs. I see him gesturing down the field as the boys embark on a workout. He has life in his stride as though he's running downcourt. But the miles take their toll and soon Lennon is humbled, his smile gone, his voice quiet. He struggles to keep up.

I'm still encouraged. Lennon's here, on the team, running. This gives me a competent sixth man. I have room to breathe. We'll have a decent sixth man to fill the gap if one of the five juniors gets hurt. And if Lennon trains hard, he can be as strong as Ryan or Brock. He's an athlete. All he has to do is try.

Lennon could learn a lesson in trying from Leschak, who never dogs a workout. Now, there's a duo. Lennon may be the cool cat, but he's also a party-liner, craving acceptance. He's parochial to the core, a creature of the Jersey Shore. Leschak is politically aware. Apropos of nothing, he brings up a drought in Africa or mocks a St. Rose school policy. I like worldliness in a cross-country runner. It shows thinking. You can't push yourself when your breathless body races the wilds without thinking about what the hell you're really doing out there.

The boys depart, fit and ready for the upcoming school term and regular, daily practices. Lennon bounces away with three St. Rose girls he's driving home. "See ya, Coach," he calls without turning around. I wave him off.

"Keep running," I say. "Keep running."

3

Coaching in Catholicville

The school term begins, and Michael Dunn, who lives nearby, skateboards to our meeting place at the lake for practice. With his portable wheels, brush crew cut and choirboy self-effacement, Dunn is like a little kid from Anywhere, USA: oblivious to the outside world. He is the first runner to show up.

"Any freshmen coming out?" Dunn asks as he hops off his board.

The other boys come by car or on foot, lugging heavy books and athletic bags stuffed with clothing and gear. Brock Silvestri asks about the freshmen, too. John Lennon and Chris Ruhl, my two seniors, smack each other playfully, falling over their bags and cursing each other innocently. Ryan Lavender picks up on Brock. "Yeah," says Ryan, as our team of eight is all assembled and fixed on the crash of September waves rustling the shore, "where are the freshmen?"

The boys respond to our plight. I go begging for freshmen. Last winter, I met prospective freshmen and their parents at a school open house, pitching cross-country as the coolest, baddest, most fail-safe school sport, and besides that—parents, are you listening?—the discipline will lead to better grades and a healthy body, mind, and spirit. I wore a shirt and tie, showed them team trophies, shook the boys' hands, looked them in the eye, and promised salvation. About 80 percent of the boys, including those with running experience, rejected my overtures, saying, "I play soccer." About 15 percent told me, "I play basketball." The other five percent had trouble walking.

Undeterred, I corralled some forty kids to write down their names on my legal pad for "having interest in cross-country." I sent all forty a follow-up letter. I called all forty to make sure they got the letter and to say hello. I sent all forty another letter when my preseason summer meeting was set for June. I called all forty again to see who was coming to the meeting. About a dozen said they'd be there. Six boys showed up.

And now, with the Running Roses' schedule of seven dual meets in the Class B Central league, four invitationals including a national meet in North Carolina, the county championships, conference championships, Catholic schools championship, and state championships—fifteen meets in all—staring us in the face, the news is loud and clear: no freshmen. Despite the team's success (last year we were 5-1 in dual meets and placed third in the state meet) and my reputation as a straight shooter who knows his running, not one of the six freshman hopefuls is on the official school roster.

If this trend continues, in another year I'll have no team.

"What are we going to do, Coach?" says Dunn.

"You run your best, that's all that matters," I say feebly while sending the boys off on their warm-up jog, about a mile, around the lake.

I would have settled for one freshman, as long as it was the Kelly boy. He was a grammar school winner, twice the size of most freshmen, and he actually spoke up and asked questions at our June meeting. Kelly wanted to know how we trained. A prize athlete for sure. He'd even impressed Lavender. "This kid is good," he said.

But Kelly is also a swimmer, and St. Rose has no boys' swim team. Girls' swimming, yes; boys', no. Kelly winds up at a public school, and when I see his solid early results in cross-country, I want to run down to the Belmar beach and scream.

With my skeletal roster of eight, I will need some bit of magic— a blessing perhaps—for us to stay in one collective piece all season. Every meet is important, and I will have to thread the needle in training the boys hard but not too hard. Unfortunately, you don't know if the training is too hard until it's too late. Suddenly, someone's knee hurts. One bad knee could wipe out our season.

I keep that reality to myself. I try to use our smallness to advantage. I tell the boys our small group will work together closely, helping one another. We'll run shoulder to shoulder, foster team strategy. Each athlete will have a key role on the team. Everyone counts. No one is expendable. Everyone must have a sense of responsibility. Don't let your teammates down.

As the boys form a circle on the grass for stretching exercises, I go on about this, repeating my words, emphasizing responsibility, looking at each boy one by one. Gallagher smiles at me. My words sail through him. Others avoid eye contact or chatter among themselves. Silvestri looks down intently. Lavender looks away. I hammer on, pounding my fist into my hand, raising my voice. "We don't need anyone else," I tell them. "We have ourselves. Run hard, do the right thing, and we'll do fine."

I razz Gallagher about his poor sit-ups and notice his tattered running shoes. I shake my head. Beaten-up shoes can cause injury, so where are the new ones I told everyone to have when school started?

"Left them at home, Coach," says Gallagher. He flashes a *you-*

know-me grin, then pipes up, "Are we doing anything on the sixteenth, Coach?" That happens to be the day of our first meet, the St. Dominic's Invitational. "I have a wedding in Ohio." I tell Gallagher, you're not going, so tell Mom and Dad now, or pack your stuff and join girls' field hockey. There can be no equivocating.

At least the boys are in fair shape. Most attended some summer practices and also ran a little on their own. I have material to work with and smack my lips for the opportunity to try to mold this group of sweet, unknowing boys into state contenders. But as a coach I realize that I, too, have to learn to pace myself or it'll be me who's broken before it's too late.

Every afternoon, when I cross the Shark River Bridge into Belmar and meet my boys at the beach, I feel a weight lifted. Personal problems recede, as though washed away in the distant waters. But that solace has been upended recently by my father, Martin, seventy-eight, who had the nerve to suffer a debilitating stroke and interfere with my cross-country season. As soon as dad took ill, my first reaction was, how will it affect *me*?

My independent streak extends to family matters. At times, I try not to get too close because with closeness comes risk. My parents, brother, and sister are usually on the same page about things, sharing the personal details of their lives. I guard my privacy, staying on the fringes, where I'm most comfortable.

Dad's stroke, which steals the life out of his right arm and leg, pummels me. At first, I barely have time to feel sorry for him. There's too much to do in ensuring proper medical care and rehab, dealing with doctors, and shuttling my mother back and forth to the hospital. One day at the hospital, when I finally begin to sort out my feelings, I walk into a dark, empty room and cry my eyes out. I weep not only for my father, but for myself: for being reminded how hard it is to expose yourself, honestly, to people you care dearly about.

For me, coaching seems to fill that need. I can show the boys my feelings without consequences. It is a kind of love, the way I bring them along, but it's on my terms. I make the rules. When the boys follow them most assiduously, running their little hearts out, I receive their love and together, as one, we make a spiritual ascent. The Immaculate Ascension.

I'm not only an authority figure but also a willing role model. These boys need worthy role models and I can tell that the St. Rose teachers, some of them clergy, may be too stiff. I reveal my emotions, show the boys how much I care, shed a tear now and then, hug them, plead with them, get pissed off at them, call them at night, ask about their grades, pace nervously at races, laugh when they're funny. I'm myself.

With gender roles in flux, I'm happy to clarify some confusion over what it means to be a man. *Look at me, I can be strong and vulnerable at once.* I want these boys to leave me not only as better runners but better people.

I want them to possess the grace Aquinas talked about, a grace I see in my father.

In time, I find my grip loosens on my rigid family autonomy, and I grab the cell phone when the guys are running to check in on Dad. Thankfully, his speech is only marginally affected by the stroke, which may have been caused by his earlier years of smoking. Dad was a marine who fought in World War II and worked hard all his life. When he retired at sixty-five, I wrote an essay in the *Times* about working with Dad on his soda truck in the summers. I said it was an honor to see "the simple greatness of a hard-working man."

In an irony that's almost spooky, who should be in charge of the hospital division that makes Dad's supportive foot appliance but Brock Silvestri's father, Bob, a specialist in this area who's able to answer many questions. I can't help but feel worn out from the daily issues that inevitably erupt around my parents all fall and am torn between family needs and my current first love: the team.

To coach at my best, I must do what I urge the boys to do: make smallness our secret weapon. I realize I have to get under each boy's skin. I have to get personal, something a large squad would not allow. I have to find the tiny, hidden desire in each boy and work that over with relentless prodding, cajoling, affirming motivation till they explode with a breakthrough performance. Or else I'll explode myself.

Most days we train at the lake and boardwalk across the street. We go to Holmdel Park weekly for the hills and because it's our primary racing site. On occasion we head to our home course, a hardscrabble thirty-acre site a few towns away. Actually, we're quite lucky. The boards, as we call them, are easy on the legs. We know the distances of various landmarks. You get a breeze off the ocean and have plenty to look at to stave off tedium. There's always an adult runner ahead to chase down, a bathroom for a pit stop, and when you reach the turnaround point halfway, you know the coach will greet you with encouragement, split times, and a water spray in your sweating face.

I send the boys off on a five-miler. They could probably do seven or eight, but I'm cautious. This is a distance day, what we use to fill in between heart-thumping, faster-paced work. My instructions: Try to run the second half faster than the first. Come back strongly. You have to in races. How you practice is how you compete. Today the command is a tall order because the boys will face a headwind after the turnaround.

They pull off their shirts and run south through Belmar to the middle of Spring Lake, and back. This is the nexus of the northern corridor of the Jersey Shore. On summer weekends, Belmar, a ticky-tack beach strip, attracts girls too big for their bikinis and beefy young guys with New York plates on their cars, their oily torsos glistening in the sun. Spring Lake, known as the Irish Riviera, has million-dollar homes and a more mature crowd. People come with the Sunday *Times* and fold it with conviction against the slapping winds.

When I station myself at the midway checkpoint, 2.5 miles, I call off times and spray each boy. With the wind at his back, Ryan leads the team in a crisp 14:30. Brock's close behind at 14:40. If they're apart, they're pushing. That's what I like to see. Mike Dunn's next at 15:45. They stick their faces into the spray, seeking relief. It's a hot day but resplendent with rich blue skies. The sun feels good. The boys are used to the heat by now. Their bodies have adapted and no longer work overtime transporting oxygen to the muscles.

"Good pace," I call out. "Excellent. Keep it up. Keep working all the way home."

I wait to see each boy, to make sure he's okay, then drive back to the finish. Before they return, I have some time to contemplate the hidden desire in each boy. For Ryan Lavender, it's the struggle for stardom in order to rise above the issues in his parents' divorce. For Brock Silvestri, it's the smart use of strength to compensate for lack of speed. For Michael Dunn, it's the courage to excel and risk failure as the youngest in a family of high-achieving older sisters. For Justin Gallagher, it's the recognition that commitment will bring reward whether or not he can satisfy his father. For Michael Solebello, it's the belief that a sprinter can run distance and conquer the tough hills of cross-country. For John Lennon, it's the maturity to know the good that running can do. For Chris Ruhl, it's the confidence to see improvement around the corner. For John Leschak, it's an appreciation of how running can enhance an artistic sensibility.

Leaning into the wind, Brock finishes first in 31 minutes. Ryan's a minute behind. I'm not surprised. Ryan loves to surge ahead, patience be damned. I'm excited because Mike Solebello made up 17 seconds on Dunn from the midpoint and they ran in together. I pat both Mikes on their moist backs as they cross our imaginary line on the boardwalk. The boys drink hard, devour the orange slices I've brought, put their shirts back on.

Fine running, but when they're done the boys don't talk much about running. I'd like to hear running in their conversation. *C'mon, guys, talk about how running feels, trade ideas, plan to meet for a Sunday practice.* They're not there yet. They veer right into baseball or basketball. Indeed, next Friday one boy misses practice to go to Boston to see the Yankees play the Red Sox. The same day, John Lennon is off on a college recruiting trip.

Whenever our trip to North Carolina comes up, no one says anything about the great competition we'll face. The boys are pitched on missing school for a day, the hotel sleeping arrangement, where they're going to eat, and mostly the girls they'll see from all over the country. They assume girls from California are like Playboy bunnies. Lennon wisecracks about his sexual prowess and gets big laughs. I try not to listen to the undertow of his remarks.

I'm still waiting for someone to greet me at practice and say, *Coach, can we do an extra couple of miles today?* Instead, Dunn can be counted on to plead, "We're not running hard today, are we, Coach?"

Running hard is not easy to contemplate. It's one more hard

thing you have to do in your day. Baseball, basketball, soccer—they offer immediate, external rewards, affirmed by every basket through the hoop, kick into the net, or pop of the ball against your glove. Running is internal and cooks slowly like a good stew. I feel that every day I have to make sure the stew simmers.

I do a lot of cooking when we go through loosening-up strides during the warm-up and cool-down. I have the boys run five fifty-yarders on the open field at the lake. I blow my whistle and they take off toward me. They're supposed to run close to full speed. I check their form and attitude. Some boys work it, others goof off. I mock the laggards, but they seem to like whatever attention they get.

"Okay, Mike Dunn's way out front, looking good."

"C'mon, Justin, work your arms, loosen your neck. Don't strain."

"Brock, use your arms, push, you're slower than the girls."

"Good, crisp leg action, Solebello. That's what I like to see."

"Look at Ryan. Nice stride, even with black socks."

"Chris, great job, but don't lean back so much. Forward lean."

"Leschak wins this one. A soph beats the juniors. Awww-rrright!"

"Sgt. Pepper, c'mon, is that Chinese food from lunch slowing you down?"

This is our foreplay. Strides set the tone for the day. Later, when we do our second set, the guys are tired, run slower and moan. But I sling more arrows, keeping them engaged, sparking smirks, and hopefully making a few points that will sink in about the correct way to run. We'll see when we start racing.

We stumble along toward our first meet a week away. Lavender gets sick and misses practice. Mike Dunn practically collapses from fatigue while running one day. I stop him and give him a ride back.

Later that night, his mom says he had a bad reaction to allergy medication. Gallagher gets a bad stomach cramp and slows to a crawl. He says he forgot to go to the bathroom before practice.

Food and digestion issues are prominent in the daily dialogue. Guys eat crap. It's not only what they eat but when. For some, school lunch is ten thirty; for others, twelve thirty. A light lunch is best, followed by an easily-digestible pre-practice snack. And don't forget to take care of business before running. I harp on proper diet and drinking plenty of water. I ask them, why compromise all the hard training by eating junk and messing up your stomach?

I suggest they eat like the great Kenyan runners, who are fortified by a cornmeal dish called ugali. "Tell your moms to pick up some ugali at Foodtown," I suggest with a straight face. One boy takes me seriously. "Coach is joking, you asshole," asserts Lennon.

Kenyans dominate almost every big race around the world. I'm starting to hear that some high school coaches around the country are training their runners "like Kenyans." Sounds like a good idea, but I wonder how truly "Kenyan" American kids can be. Maybe we'll find out in North Carolina, where the nation's top teams will congregate.

We continue training like Jerseyans. On a day for long intervals, the bread-and-butter of cross-country training, I assign the boys three turns of a hard mile. It's run a hard mile, jog three minutes, run a second hard mile, jog three minutes, run a third hard mile, and you're done. We run back and forth on the boardwalk. I hustle in my car to call out splits and good cheer. The kids enjoy the challenge, and they like knowing their times at the end. They can see tangible progress.

This workout is about as tough as a race, so I can see what the team pecking order looks like. I see toughness, too, and weakness.

Who sticks with whom. Who gives up, goes through the motions. Who runs smart, trying for even pace, as I urge. Who has a ready excuse, or a killer instinct. The mile is actually little short because we mark it where the boardwalk stops in South Belmar and you have to run on the open road before the boards resume in Spring Lake. If my fastest boy hits close to five minutes per 0.9 mile, I'll be satisfied.

Lavender's still out sick, a shame since Brock will have to push on his own. Lavender gets frequent colds, which I attribute to his parents' split. He seems to be carrying a heavy burden. He's got a younger sister and is sort of the man of the house at the moment. Both his parents have new romantic interests. Emotions are raw. I feel that I should step in and try to help, but I'm wary about sticking my nose where it doesn't belong.

Mike Dunn, not Brock, comes into view first, leading the opening mile. Woooooo! I love it! Dunn's alive! Every so often, Dunn shows his true colors. His protests notwithstanding, the boy can run. His face is red and his expression blank. I always urge Dunn "to run with authority." He's doing it now. "Great, you're running with authority, Michael Dunn. I knew you could do it."

I call out the times: 5:08 for Dunn, 5:13 for Brock and Solebello, 5:17 for Gallagher, 5:28 for Lennon, 5:29 for Leschak, 5:30 for Ruhl. The last three guys are in over their heads and will slow drastically. With continuing great weather, they get sucked in, but they'll pay. Dunn leads the second mile in 5:27. Brock's on his shoulder in 5:28. Solebello and Gallagher are close to 6:00, Lennon at 6:30, Leschak and Ruhl over 7:00.

"Attaboy, attaboy, attaboy, great job, one more to go, that's all, one more to go, c'mon, tough it out, you're almost done, one more hard one, pace yourself, elbows in, good knee lift, dig into the wind, stick together, c'mon, stick together, team running, that's what it's all about, team running, don't let your teammate down, stick together . . ."

Brock and Dunn finish the third mile together in 5:24. "Togetherness," I shout. "I love it." Solebello improves to 5:43, Gallagher hangs on in 5:59, but should be way up there—frankly, with Dunn. Gallagher's got so much more to give. About twice a season, he breaks out of his shell. Lennon, Leschak, and Ruhl are over 7:00.

The boys cool off and I assess the effort. I have a good word for everyone, even Lennon, who looks pretty raggedy. I rave more about Dunn. I use his effort to make a point for all. I brush my hand over Dunn's bristly head. Solebello, craving his share of the plaudits, breaks the guys' post-workout quiet.

"Coach, I felt pretty good. I think my legs are getting stronger. I was happy with my last mile," he offers.

"So was I, Mike. You showed you can be up with the front guys before long." It's an opening to zero in on Gallagher. "Justin, Solebello pulled away from you in the last mile. You just let him go? Mike's a sprinter, and he pulled away from you. Jeez. I see Mike moving up on the team. Justin, you keep losing ground and you'll be nowhere at Holmdel."

Holmdel Park is the context for everything. Every remark, every time comparison, every gain or loss in strength, every change in attitude, missed practice, school detention, or bad-lunch-induced side stitch. It's all about Holmdel, because that's where eight of our fifteen meets will be run, including the state championship, and when you put down a time on Holmdel's hilly 5K course, every runner in the state, from Wildwood to Whippany, knows what it means. Your Holmdel time brands you.

When I pull a boy aside, like I did with Mike Dunn after his marvelous practice, I focus on Holmdel and say, "Mike, last year you ran 18:26 at Holmdel. This season, you should be at least a minute faster." I lean in closer to his face. "Mike, 17:30 or better. That's you. Run like that and we can win states."

I won't let up. That night, I call Dunn's house and speak to his mom. I tell her how well her son did today, how much we're counting on him. "Oh my," says Mary Dunn. "How nice." Mike's an honor student, but because he's short and comes off young, he's unsure of himself and self-conscious in the pseudo-hip school crowd. The word on the street is, show me a talented runner with a poor self-image and I'll show you a future champion. From the street's mouth to God's ears.

A year ago, I came closer than ever to the Christian God on behalf of John Leschak, then a freshman, when he competed in his second meet. State rules prohibit athletes from wearing jewelry in competition and Leschak, being new, came to race with a cross around his neck. On the starting line, an official ordered him to remove the chain and Leschak handed it to me for safekeeping.

I'd never actually held a Catholic cross before. I put the cross in my pocket and decided to touch it on behalf of John, hoping some good luck might come his way. Though not a natural runner, Leschak was working hard, pushing more than many of the older kids. John runs with an odd gait: short, choppy stride and accentuated arm action. He looks like a windup toy. Leschak exists outside the box, and I considered his funny stride another example of his personal style.

In his first race, Leschak had committed a classic freshman error. He started out way too fast in the crowd, caught the rig early on (that's rigor mortis, or severe muscle failure), and had to drop out.

After that, John almost quit the team in embarrassment. I built him back up, but he experienced chest pains in practice (the mind-body effect, I assumed) and was sidelined for weeks until medical tests determined there was nothing wrong with him.

So I held John's cross in his comeback race. He needed to succeed or I feared we'd lose him for good. That meant one thing: finishing. There was no other goal. I'd ordered John to start slowly and pace himself. I told him his place didn't matter. Man, just get to the finish line.

As John ran, I found myself clutching the cross in prayer for him. Considering the fusion of the two religions on our team, I decided to recite a Hebrew prayer of healing to myself as I held the cross. It was the tender *Mishebeirach*, asking God for renewal of body and soul, recited at all synagogues. I raced around the course as I always do, keeping tabs on John, imploring him to monitor his pace. John not only finished but beat some opposing runners and came within a few seconds of sticking with Chris Ruhl. Still, I returned the cross with mixed emotions.

They were the same emotions I always feel walking into the St. Rose school building. What am I, a card-carrying Jew, doing in a Catholic school? If in my youth I fought against peer pressure to hold dearly to a faith that I understood even then was somehow exalted and true, what am doing in Catholicville? Some of the students and teachers probably assume I am Catholic. And those who know I'm Jewish may think I can't be much of a Jew, because what would a good Jew be doing in a place where crucifixes stare down from every wall? What if they knew I'd clutched one in my hand.

Even with I-passed-for-Catholic conflicts, though, I feel spiritual reinforcement at St. Rose. While it's not my religion in the walls, there is a collective goodness in the building that makes me feel connected, fueling my passion for the team. The school has become something of a home.

I mix well with the faculty, nodding, shaking hands, chatting with other coaches. The sisters know a Jew when they see one and regard me with wonder and, I sense, just a wee bit of disdain. The mood in the building is subdued and earnest, but also insulated and protective. The school feels like a dated, closed society, a kind of sanctuary against the cruel, debased world. Passing the classrooms, I notice decorum and learning but little you would call educational vibrancy.

The teachers I meet seem caring and satisfied. Though they are poorly paid, they don't have to deal with the discipline issues rampant in public schools. They get automatic respect, or at least cooperation. At St. Rose, any troublemaker is thrown out.

The school opened in 1923. The current edifice was built in 1956. St. Rose is noted for its sizable gym, rebuilt after a 1980 fire, and the school hosts various basketball tournaments. The weight room is tiny, the library inadequate. There is a small chapel that I peek into. When I arrive for practice, the cafeteria is cleaned spotless, and the coolest kids hang out there after class trying to score points with the opposite sex.

Older boys who quit the cross-country team say hello, Mr. Bloom, how's the team making out? Great, Kevin, what's new with student council? The girls are cute and virginal and upright in their pleated skirts and white blouses. A few choose to be daring with makeup, blouse buttons open, and a womanly demeanor. I catch some furtive female glances, and I can't tell if it's the Jewish thing or whether my fit-and-lean, un-teacher-like look is a shock. A few girls make me think risqué thoughts, but of course I don't let on.

The principal, Michele Campbell, a layperson, always gives me a big hello. She likes how I nurture the boys, and she knows running. The athletic director, my boss, is a big, burly man, Dick Alger, a former wrestling coach who succeeded Mike Robertson. Dick's a sweet guy who always looks overburdened. He seems content knowing little about running. Dick and I get along, but it's hard for me to feel he's on my side. My requests—say, for bus transportation to practice at Holmdel Park—seem to vex him. I decide that it's best for me to handle as much as possible on my own and try to stay out of his hair. I assume that team success will smooth the way. Not really. Even when we pile up victories, Dick is too busy with the other sports to care that much about cross-country.

Crucifixes aside, the evenhanded Catholic quiet of St. Rose is strangely comforting to me. I've never clicked with Jewish *tummeling* and don't think I've ever told a joke. I can be in a roomful of people with my father and the two of us will say nothing for hours. But I won't let go of the Reform Jewish commandment to repair the world, known as *tikkun olam*. I figure that since Christian kids are taught that suffering along with Jesus on the cross is a sanctifying duty, when you combine my nurturing energy with boys who should welcome pain you've got the makings of one fine cross-country team.

Change of scenery keeps the boys fresh, so we venture to Holmdel Park. With school buses at a premium, I have the two seniors with driver's licenses shuttle the others, and with me driving, too, we're covered. Kids driving kids scares the shit out of me. I have parents sign an authorization form, but will the student drivers—John Lennon and Chris Ruhl—do the right thing? I can only hope. I deliver a stern message: We go together, and we drive below the 65 mph speed limit.

It's a half-hour drive, and within minutes, past a toll on the

Garden State Parkway, I've lost the guys. Or have they lost me? I freak out, assume they've sped away and do eighty to try to catch them. They're nowhere. They beat me to the park. Seeing me fuming, they guard their smiles and say they were looking for me, where was I? I yell in the parking lot: "Pull that nonsense again and we stay home."

No Holmdel? That's funny. I keep an angry face and send the boys on their warm-up. Let them giggle their way through it. I ponder the nightmare of a car accident and grow angrier. My wife, Andrea, who's not keen on my coaching to begin with, gets furious when I tell her I drive the boys. She can't believe that's allowed and says if anything happens the parents will sue us and we'll be destitute. I dunno, I just want to coach.

Since I rarely blow my top, the boys know when I mean it. We're all business as I send the team on three continuous circuits of the 2.1-mile freshman course for a total of 6.3 miles, substantial running considering the hills and the quick tempo I ask for. Ryan is back from a sickbed but still not himself; he jogs for half an hour. Brock's getting sharper—his baseball buns from the summer are all gone—but he has no one to push him and even though he's our fastest guy by far, he sags on the third loop.

This day belongs to Mike Solebello, the sprinter. I keep working on his mind. "You're a distance runner," I tell him. Distance, distance, distance. Brock's got nothing on you. With your speed, you can run rings around him." Brock smiles. He knows I'm mixing apples and oranges. Solebello's sprint speed means little in cross-country, which is based mostly on strength and the aerobic system.

But Solebello listens and says, "I feel it coming, Coach. The hills didn't bother me. I wasn't that tired." Solebello ran the circuits in 15:58, 17:00, and 15:56. He gave in to fatigue on the middle loop, letting others gap him. But I keep that to myself. Let Mike enjoy the moment.

Solebello has an elegant stride but he keeps his shoulders too high, tightening his upper body. I can't let that go. "Don't forget to relax your shoulders," I say. "You're still too tight."

Sgt. Pepper's coming around, too. He looks like half a runner. I've got two months to forge the second half. That goal is undermined when Lennon's father, John, comes by after practice and pulls me aside. He tells me that John is being recruited by colleges for basketball and will have to miss some meets because of "obligations." John has to play in tournaments for the exposure. And he has to visit schools. His mother feels he's losing weight because of running, weakening him for basketball. The father, a Port Authority policeman, says they have to pursue a possible free ride to college.

What can I say? Basketball or cross-country, it's no contest.

In my mind, we're now a team of seven. I expect Lennon will drift away before the state meet. Our varsity is set: the five juniors who will carry the squad to the end, plus the soph Leschak and the senior Ruhl, both on the slow side of average. We will no longer have a strong sixth man in a pinch. If one of my top five gets a sniffle at the wrong time, we're history.

To prevent untimely sniffles, I space out the hard running, assuring adequate rest. With St. Dominic's coming up on Saturday, our last hard workout before competition is on Wednesday, and we make our first visit to our home course, the St. Rose Athletic Field, a twenty-minute drive away in Wall Township. Ryan Lavender, finally well, rides with me.

Normally reticent, Ryan opens up, talking about his auspicious goals. He wants to be one of the best runners in New Jersey, maybe even beyond. My reaction is, "Bravo, but how are you going to get there? You're simply not running enough. Over the summer, you cared more about lifeguarding than running. You logged maybe two hundred miles. You need to log five hundred miles next summer, how about it?"

Ryan is intrigued with the aura of success, and he's too smart not to understand how meager his effort is thus far. But he's not connecting the dots. It's as though he's talked himself into believing he can excel, but when he starts to get close he sabotages himself with some goofy misstep. I sense that his family situation has left him without an anchor, and that he's floating in some vague existence that has him up one day and down the next. In one sense, the team's embrace is saving Ryan; in another, the team represents an ideal that Ryan may be too shattered to grasp.

Ryan's parents are involved, individually, with the team. I speak to both Karen and Dennis but so far the divorce issue is in the background. Ryan does not bring up his family to me and I'm afraid to say the wrong thing.

As a freshman, the boy ran like a dream and was named all-state for the freshman class. I thought I had a star on my hands. Last year, as a soph, Ryan never got traction. He won some races and led St. Rose, but in the big meets he'd either go out too fast and die or struggle from the outset. His best time at Holmdel was 17:22, only thirty-six seconds faster than he'd run as a freshman. I was bewildered, frustrated, almost angry. Ryan should have run 16:30 and won the state championship in our division. After he took sixth, following his third place from the previous year, I started to blame myself for not training Ryan hard enough.

Our home-course site is a patchwork of fields for soccer and field hockey with running trails through a backwoods section that abuts a small airport. The trails are sandy and uneven, a minefield for turned ankles. We stay on the flat, grass fields for our workout, which is ten fast runs of sixty seconds alternated with ten slow runs for recovery. Sixty seconds fast, sixty seconds slow. There are no measured distances so we have to run on time. I set up cones around the soccer field so our path is like a track.

A fast minute is close to a quarter mile. It's short enough for you to run very fast, but too long for top speed. By repeating the effort with short recovery, you tax the body while your pulse is still fairly high, giving you the redline feeling you can expect in racing. Your body and mind learn to tolerate more and more stress. You increase the capacity of the blood to carry oxygen to fuel the working muscles. And you learn guts.

You also learn proper pacing. Start out too fast for the first couple of runs and you'll crash. The idea is even pace, just like a race, so that hopefully you'll run the tenth hard minute with the same authority—"run with authority, Michael Dunn"—as the first. I drum home this point as the boys shake out the last kinks in their legs.

My whistle sends them on their first run, and everyone seems to get the point but one: Ryan Lavender. Most of the group is clustered. Brock smartly holds back just a touch. Ryan, however, is flying like a madman. He's way ahead, his legs churning, his strawberry hair whipped back by the wind, his countenance intent. When he passes me around the circle, I'm too stunned to say a word. "Good pace," I call to the group behind him.

After sixty seconds, I blow the whistle. Time to jog. "Ease off, Ryan, you've got nine to go. Don't kill yourself." He jogs by himself, seemingly proud to be ahead. Actually, I want Ryan to wipe out. He must learn a lesson, and the other boys must see it. You can't be that reckless and succeed. And if Ryan can run like that for the whole workout, more power to him, he is indeed championship material.

Second run, same thing. Ryan's screaming ahead, the other guys hanging back. During the resting jog, I check faces. Ryan's tired but won't show it. The others look more composed and I think I detect some chatter about Ryan's foolishness, or, rather, his ego. Like, *Who does he think he is?*

By the fifth hard minute, Ryan's practically crawling. Brock passes him evenly. The others are moving in on him. For the moment, I decide to say nothing to Ryan. Let him suffer. I compliment the rest of the boys on their patience, and in fact it's a very good workout with strong running evidenced to the tenth and last repetition. We'll be ready to race on Saturday.

Ryan's last runs are a survival shuffle and he's embarrassed. His mistake is too brazen for me to handle privately. We've been around the block on this before, so there's little to say. I gather the boys and announce up front that Ryan knows what he did wrong and everyone witnessed it. Ryan nods his head yes. My tone is that this pacing business is elementary, you guys are experienced and should know what to do, right? I find a positive spin by telling Ryan his mistake was a gift, a bit of fate. Better to screw up now than in a race, right?

Now, you're not going to make the same fatal mistake on Saturday when we go up against Christian Brothers Academy and other state powers, right?

4

Our Time Is Now

The season's first meet has me on edge. On the team bus to Jersey City, I fidget with the *Times*, sip coffee, try to relax. I glance back from my front seat to check on the kids. I try to gauge their moods. I look for Ryan and Brock, my big guns. Are they conversant or quiet, excited or indifferent? Do they look ready to race? How would I know? Is there a *way* to look ready to race? I search for a hint, perhaps a rousing comment about the race we're going to run—a race that, like all races, will take everything you have. It's a lovely Saturday morning, guys, and soon you will have to spill your guts out on the cross-country course.

They seem okay with that. I have my doubts. These are doubts I can trace to my own high school running. In my youth, I was fast. In my Brooklyn neighborhood, we marked off one hundred yards in crayon down the street so we could race. I'd give friends a head start, catch them by the seventy, and laugh across the finish. My churning legs never gave way. Running fast was transcendent, an out-of-body experience.

Speed became my identity. I immersed myself in track, followed the champions, and trekked to meets in Madison Square Garden. Running became my refuge, armor against what I saw as the inevitable harshness of life.

I was like some science nerd who spent all his time fascinated with bugs. Teenage mating games turned me off and I withdrew from the social scene. Better to pore over my track stats, my bugs. I was drawn to the decisiveness of running performances and mainly, I think, the fact that running success was based solely on you. Running was the one thing in life you could actually control. If you ran and practiced, you got better. I saw a pristine clarity in the advancement.

I remember reading in the papers in February, 1960, that Jim Grelle of Oregon was the winner of the mile in the Millrose Games indoor track meet at Madison Square Garden. His time was 4:06.4, one-tenth of a second faster than Ron Delaney's winning time the year before. Those numbers impressed my young mind. They made me think, if you want to improve it's up to you, try harder.

That very same month, I received my Bar Mitzvah at my grandfather's shul. It was my mother's father, Grandpa Sam. He stood at my side, mouthing the words with me, as I recited the Hebrew text. With Grandpa's voice in my ear, it was hard to follow the passages and avoid an embarrassing miscue. I was already nervous at an unfamiliar synagogue. But the occasion had to be celebrated at Grandpa's shul because he and Grandma would not drive on the Sabbath. This piety was to be respected without question. The "more Jewish" you were, the better. The more you sacrificed, the more you held tradition in awe, the better you were. Being Jewish, you were accountable. You couldn't just live, you had to *be*.

Be *what*? I cleaved to the idea of Jewish goodness—"redemption of the human race," as Israel's first prime minister, David Ben-Gurion, had put it. But I feared the weight of greater responsibility linked to the recent calamity in Europe. That seemed too heavy a burden. Jewish joy always seemed mixed with Jewish lament. Contentment was fragile, even foolish; there were monstrous remains of a world gone mad just around the corner. And no one to help. You were alone.

I needed an outlet, a way to live while absorbing the hard issues at my own pace. I pulled back the curtains, opened the windows, and breathed in the fresh air of running. Now, on the school bus rumbling along the New Jersey Turnpike, I am still seeking refuge from the meaner streets and still wishing hard for things perhaps unattainable as I snap open the window latch to inhale Saturday morning.

Years ago in Italy, writing about the 1988 Olympic marathon champion Gelindo Bordin, I was stuck by Bordin's melancholy as he described the climax of his gold-medal run in Seoul. "Saturday is better than Sunday," Bordin told me. "It comes from the poem, 'Sabato del Villagio' ['Saturday in the Village']." Bordin explained that the deliverance of victory was like the joy of preparing for Sunday, the holiday, but then Monday would come and with it the mundane realities of ordinary life.

Bordin's sentiment touches me as I contemplate the day's agenda. Nothing is steeped with more promise than a high school sports contest on a Saturday morning. Yet, at Saturday meets, I do feel a tug of ambiguity. Almost no one is Jewish. I am swimming in the gentile world of my choosing. It's the Sabbath and I wonder if I should be in prayer with Jews at services. I wonder if I should be wrestling with Jewish issues and saying Kaddish, as the rabbi intones, "for the six million." My wife and I go to temple on Friday nights, but on Saturday, God's day of rest and reflection, I am hard at work coaching Catholic kids on running.

I wonder if my coaching style is merely a convenient, nonthreatening way to express Jewish values, to dabble at the surface without confronting head-on the complex and piercing issues of Jewish existence in a post-Holocaust world. Or are my modest efforts worthy of the continuum of Jewish life, a touchstone for now, leading to more weighty spiritual growth later on?

I think back to Grandpa Sam, who owned a butcher shop in a Brooklyn neighborhood now exclusively orthodox. There, on the Sabbath, that world stops. People pray and stick together as Jews in a world that, still, would just as soon do away with us. When I was growing up, my mother, Jeanette, spoke to her parents as a lifeline every day. They conversed in Yiddish, which seemed like a secret code. I got wise to some of the expressions. But I also grew to be on guard for such closeness, especially after Grandma and Grandpa got sick and died. For periods during their last days, they were cared for in our home. The sounds of grave illness kept me awake at night. The ordeal tore my mother to pieces, and I, too, absorbed such losses for the long haul.

Running on the high school team was my rock. However, in my longing for success and the comfort of that invigorating, baggage-free world—in the vague recognition that running could be my only hope—I gave my track exploits too much weight, hurting my efforts. Before each race, I plunged into a numbing, strength-sapping fear, something like I feel now as we cross the no-name bridge into Jersey City and unload at Lincoln Park for the St. Dominic's Cross Country Invitational.

"How ya doing, Coach?" Solebello calls. "You all right?"

It never occurs to me that the guys would sense my anxiety. I can't allow that. I have to be like I tell the boys to be: confident, optimistic, clear thinking, unruffled by the challenge, looking forward to this first test of fitness.

I tell Mike I'm fine, how are you. I clap my hands, bring out a smile, and say, it's going to be a great day, let's get ready. Each season, the first meet is like a new day. A coach's hope and calculation have not yet been undone. Everything is on the table. I can fantasize about my top five boys running to the level they should, without any history to say otherwise. No one has let himself or me down, yet. The world is open.

The weather is cool and sunny, ideal for running, and the small park fills with teams lugging their stuff. Team managers carry huge watercoolers like those you see on football fields. We have no such thing. I bring orange slices like my high school coach did for us. The sponsoring school offers a bake sale to raise money. Doughnuts, cookies, and cake are spread on tables like Easter chocolates in Neuchâtel.

Doughnuts are hardly food to run on, except when the coach says so. Two days before, as a reward for their training, I brought a box of Dunkin Donuts to practice. I must say, the boys were overwhelmed by the gesture. Of course, they bickered over who would choose first. I decided it would be based on who had the fastest times. Not very democratic but logical. Chocolate cream was the big seller. The boys left practice with full stomachs and a good feeling. So did I.

That day, we'd practiced at Holmdel Park. With the meet coming up, I ordered a medium-hard workout that included repeat runs of the quarter-mile-or-so section off the start. With Ryan Lavender still mired in impatience, I wanted to review the Saturday race plan to hold back at the outset, conserve energy, and run even pace. This is perhaps the hardest lesson for a young runner to learn. When you hold back, it seems as though you're granting opponents an advantage. But it's just the opposite: You're letting others make the mistake, which will catch up with them midway. Smart pacing takes confidence, patience, and maturity. How many seventeen-year-olds have all *that*?

Some evidence of the team's evolving maturity comes as a stunning surprise. One day at practice, as I have the boys line up for some speedwork, Brock Silvestri pipes up and says, "Coach, this has nothing to do with your coaching . . . but shouldn't we be doing a lot more distance runs?"

Bless you, son. Apparently, Brock has been scouring training theory as he does batting averages. I seize the opportunity to explain that now, as juniors, you can shoulder more intense training—speed—while in the past, as freshmen and sophs, you did mostly distance, which is less taxing. "Your bodies are getting stronger," I say. "You can handle the speed."

Ideal training combines distance with speed. We do five-mile and six-mile runs for endurance. These efforts strengthen heart function and improve oxygen flow from the blood to the muscles—your aerobic capacity. These runs also train the mind to tackle our shorter race distance, the 5K, or 3.1 miles, with confidence. Speedwork, like repeated short runs with little rest, trains the body to tolerate hard efforts with less oxygen feeding the muscles. That hurts. But racing hurts. This more intense work helps elevate your anaerobic threshold—the point at which lack of oxygen causes leg-tiring lactic acid to build in the muscles.

I explain this to the boys. I don't shun the science. They can grasp it. Brock and Mike Dunn are honor-roll students. Ryan wants to learn more. Brock listens intently, proud, I think, that the coach can discuss training methods.

I consider his question a breakthrough for the team. It took courage on many levels for Brock to challenge me. He had to know what he was talking about, articulate his concern fairly, and absorb whatever response I might have. And he had to do it in front of peers who, perhaps a short time ago, would have mocked him for being too brainy or trying to butter up the coach. But teammate approval was not an issue. Brock sensed the guys were mature enough to stand by him.

There are lessons for me, too: I take the open discussion about our training as a sign of the boys' growing faith in me. Brock seems to have a better fix than I do on team attitudes. His message is worth considering. Maybe the boys do need more distance. Maybe I'm letting them off too easy. The St. Dominic's meet will provide some answers.

Are we ready to live up to our preseason billing? The local weekly, the *Coast Star*, trumpets our chances in its fall preview. "Their Time Is Now," reads the headline. Yes, our five sophomores from last season are all back for their junior year. Our starting lineup, as the paper put it, is intact. As the boys go through their warm-ups at Lincoln Park, Michael Dunn says he wishes they could still run in the soph division. After two years of running in freshman and soph races, this is the group's first varsity race in a major invitational. Precocity is over. They're in the bigtime now.

With Christian Brothers Academy in the meet, there can be no doubt about it. CBA's entry draws reporters from the *Star-Ledger* and other papers. The CBA runners, nicknamed the Colts, jog around like they own the place. My boys look them over. I try not to notice. When someone remarks in a self-mocking manner that we're going to beat CBA, I raise my voice and say, "They're just like you: Catholic kids with freckles."

I doubt we'll touch CBA, but if you concede to one team, you'll concede to others. I'm still edgy. I'm just as anxious as the boys for the race to get started. The first meet sets the tone for the season. We've been training for three months. We've made sacrifices. We've grown. The moment has arrived. I want to see smart running and competitive fierceness. I want to see the boys hold a hard pace and push through pain. No giving up, no wishing it was over, as I did when I ran in school.

Everyone's here except for John Lennon, who's got a basketball date. In his place. I add senior Chris Ruhl to the varsity lineup. The soph, John Leschak, is in the junior varsity race by himself. I remind Leschak to remove his studded chains and bracelets or he'll be disqualified. No earrings, either. "Like what am I supposed to do, Coach?" Leschak asks. I tell him to start slow and finish fast. He does and finishes in a little over 22 minutes, a good time for him.

Many parents have turned out. They hover around the edges with cameras and coffee, giving me and their sons a wide berth. "Beautiful day, Coach," says Dennis Lavender, Ryan's dad. Dennis runs himself and I've joined him on the boards a few times. His ex, Karen, comes separately with her boyfriend. This worries me. I can't let Ryan's instability compromise the team. Karen brings cookies for the boys as a post-race treat. Dennis hangs with his brother, Mike, who's got a daughter on the team.

We do our final stride-outs to limber up. I try to rouse some emotion but no one seems up for that. I once wrote an article on a study of pre-race mental state that researchers called "Zone of Optimal Function." They found that while most athletes liked to create a relaxed state of mind before racing, others preferred to rev themselves up. This finding contradicted the view that everyone needed to be composed and meditative right before competition. My boys do tend toward the quiet mind-set.

When they're on the starting line, I take notice of how other teams act in the final moments before racing. CBA huddles in a rugby-style embrace and one boy, presumably the captain, screams them into an aggressive frenzy. Any doubt that CBA is going to kick ass has been eliminated.

I aim for a more subdued but no less meaningful tack. I remind the boys to pray. When I started coaching, I figured it was right for Catholic school boys to pray before their events. I had some vague notion that simply being Catholic was a factor in running success—I'd witnessed Catholic schools' running excellence for so long—and that prayer would reinforce the strength the boys gathered from spiritual conviction.

Fear nothing with prayer behind you. I want the boys to know I feel that way.

"Okay, let's pray," I remind them. They close ranks and Ruhl, the senior, leads them as always in a "Hail Mary," adding at the end, "Pray for us." I stand apart. It's not my prayer, and I don't want to intrude on their Catholic union. This is their time to stand on their own, and stand together, forging a commitment to run not only for themselves, but hopefully for one another and, if you will, for God.

Prayer sanctifies the effort, recognizing a higher power while enforcing the nobility of the cause. I feel our team prayer is a declaration of humanity, asserting that "we" not "they"—not Hollywood's cheap-and-easy—matter most in determining our important influences.

The boys need no prodding to pray in public, to petition God for strength. It warms me to see how they unite and announce their Catholic selves even with opposing squads at their side. Each team prayer is like money in the bank. Our account grows with commitment to be played out on the running field.

On a recent trip to cover a race in Arizona, I was impressed with the role of prayer and the spiritual aura fostered by the organizing group of Native Americans. Before a 5K in the mountains around Flagstaff, a leader had the field face east, toward the rising sun, stand in silence, and offer a prayer for anyone in need, especially those unable to run. I competed that day and prayed for my father, who needs help walking after his stroke. The leader then had us face the start with arms extended and palms open, to accept God's blessing. It was a solemn moment, adding to my spiritual reservoir.

I draw the line at the practice of thanking God, and God only, for a victory, as some athletes do. That's too Bible Belt for my taste. When I hear that sentiment from the mouths of high school runners, it sounds rehearsed and transparent. Should any St. Rose boys be fortunate enough to win anything this fall, I'll deal with their thankfulness then.

With the St. Dominic's starter in position ahead of the field and the race a minute away, I try to ease tension by mocking the boys' black socks. That's their way of being different and cool. I'll buy it. I shake each boy's hand, look him in the eye, and urge, "Smart and strong. Don't forget: smart and strong. Even pace. Don't go out too fast. Conserve. Run together. Stick with teammates. You're ready. Have fun . . ."

With my heart thumping, I dash down the path to a strategic position on the course. I want the athletes to see and hear me at key points in the race. I've found that my rallying cry can spark kids to run better. Other coaches do the same.

This is an ideal course for a first meet. It's longer than a 5K by a few hundred yards, an extra strengthening component. And instead of one meandering tour, the course is three equal loops, which facilitates proper pacing and affords me a chance to assess performances lap by lap.

The gun cracks and the field unfolds like a cavalry charge down the opening straightaway. Parents and coaches hug the narrow strip. There are twenty-five teams, more than 150 runners. I want to see my boys knitted as a team with small gaps between them. That's how you win. All five must come through. A school can take the first four places, but if the fifth and final scorer is far back, the tally will be over one hundred points, probably shy of victory.

As the runners pass me after a minute out, it's one pack, with my five key guys well placed, looking relaxed, and Ruhl hanging off the back. I shout each boy's name and say something affirmative. Then, collectively: "Attaway, St. Rose. Good positioning." Ryan and Brock are shoulder to shoulder with the leaders, who control the pace. Brock's face does not give him away. Ryan has a certain wildness in his eyes. His right arm lists to the side, like the marathon star Bill Rodgers' arm used to.

The field snakes to the route's outer reaches and I can only wait at my spot, squinting at the receding figures. I look for our purple school colors and Ryan's hair. I see him up front with a big, lurching stride, a sign of strain. Brock's back around thirtieth. The others are behind but close enough. It looks good but it's early.

My biggest challenge is forging teamwork. Everything I do must be aimed, ultimately, at team running. Commitment, pride, honor, and sacrifice must coalesce into team unity. The goal of team running is concrete: getting the boys to race as birds fly. But its underpinning is elusive and hard to define: getting the boys to link as comrades and feel responsibility for one another's success. I consider teamwork a kind of perfection because perhaps its mandate can never be fully realized. Am I trying for the impossible?

"Every team is a stage setting, a place to act out the drama in one's life," writes Joe Newton, a winning Illinois high school coach, in his excellent book *Coaching Cross Country Successfully.* "Forty years of coaching have proved to me, over and over again, that the complex inner rhythms of teamwork—flows of ambition, power, cooperation, and emotion—are the keys to making dreams come true."

Before I started coaching, I would have dismissed Newton's words as jock-speak better left in the locker room. But the man's right. I read his prescriptions and think, *Yeah, that's us, that's St. Rose.* Newton explains further, "A team needs a covenant, an agreement that binds people together. Sometimes a covenant is written out in great detail. Sometimes it is unspoken, completely expressed through actions or trust."

Completing their first circuit, the runners, now in single file, come off a short hill and pass the waiting crowd. Ryan's fifth. "Shit," I mutter to myself. He's ahead of all the CBA kids, who, together, look so darn cool about a hundred yards farther back. "What's he doing?" Dennis Lavender calls to me. We run to the roped-off path to give Ryan an earful. "Ease off, Ryan, ease off. No hurry. Long way to go."

But the boy is already in trouble. Start out too fast by even a little and your body uses too much energy very quickly and goes into overdrive. There's no way to reverse it. My cries are aimed at damage control. Father and coach commiserate. "I just hope he can hang on," I tell Dennis.

Brock's around twentieth. Mike Dunn, Justin Gallagher, and Mike Solebello are spread out in the middle. Gallagher should be on Dunn's heels. Damn. I try to determine where we are as a team. Morristown has three guys among the leaders and could challenge

CBA for the win. I think we're about fifth. I scream at Gallagher, probing for his fierceness. "Go after Dunn, go after Dunn. He's up ahead. Don't settle."

I won't settle, but this has to go both ways, man.

In the distance, I see Lavender fading. Brock's moving up. The others are steady. Ruhl's doing all right. He's comfortable knowing he'll be among the last to finish. No one pretends otherwise. On the second tour, Ryan is fifteenth with Brock on his shoulder. CBA, gradually moving up, fills the top ten and will be a certain winner. "C'mon, Ryan," I call weakly. "C'mon . . ."

I save my voice for Gallagher, who's gained a step or two on Dunn. "That's it, that's it, go for more. You can get him. Dunn's right up ahead. Don't settle. Don't settle."

I'm convinced that on the whole Gallagher's holding back. Other than his grinning give-and-take over sit-ups, Gallagher says little. At practice, his countenance and demeanor rarely change. He runs in the middle, lets other beat him, seems indifferent. Now and then his father, Larry, comes by, his clothing stained by a day of painting homes. He knows when his son is goofing off and alternates between a tenderness in understanding teenage angst and a desire to kick Justin's butt. Seems like the right balance.

The other day at practice Justin ran away from everyone on a five-mile run. He said nothing, just ran. I told the guys to run a moderate pace. Justin flew. He came in by himself in under thirty minutes. He didn't seem that tired at the end. I waited till he grabbed a drink and cooled off before saying anything. I wanted Justin to savor the moment. Finally, I said, "How about doing that in races?" No comment. No smile, either.

Down the homestretch, Gray Reinhard from Morristown wins in 17:35, CBA packs beautifully in a textbook lesson for all, and

Brock, executing well, comes in fifteenth in 18:16. Ryan staggers to the line in 18:27, twenty-third place. Dunn is not far behind him, 18:48 in thirty-ninth . . . and here comes Gallagher . . . yes, yes . . . Gallagher . . . I call his name so everyone can hear. He charges on Dunn with a wonderful kick to place forty-second, only two seconds behind in 18:50. "That's where you should be," I tell him as he heaves past the line. "Next time you beat Dunn." I don't care if Dunn hears that. He knows my intent.

"Where's Solebello? Where's our fifth man?" Mike finally appears grimacing. A 5K is long enough for our resident sprinter, and the extra yardage hits him hard. Still, he's fifty-fourth, twenty seconds behind Gallagher. Not bad at all. Ruhl brings up the rear in 20:48, much better than his time last year.

The end brings relief. When we run well, I feel energized and spread that energy around. The boys sip water. Sweat pours off them. "Great job. Great job." I recite each boy's name. The parents close in. We all brush shoulders. Ryan sits by himself, taking off his spikes. Ryan knows he should have led the team. He should have run thirty seconds faster and placed in the top five. If he'd shown patience—as Brock did—he would have been able to let his superior ability flourish on the last lap. Then our team would have had a complete performance.

I pull Ryan aside, stand face to face, grab him by the shoulders and tell him so. "Yeah . . . ," he says looking away. I tell him he can have a great season, the team can have a great season. Be patient. Do what Brock does. There's no way Brock should be ahead of you. Brock ran smart, why can't you?

The announcement comes: It's CBA first with 67 points, Morristown second with 89, Notre Dame third with 104, and St. Rose fourth with 147. I'm pleased with that. There were twenty-five schools in the race. Our scoring spread, the gap between the first man (Brock) and fifth man (Mike Solebello) is fifty-four seconds. That shows fairly tight team running. Less than a minute is considered good. CBA's spread is forty-two seconds.

Addressing the group, I pick Gallagher to highlight for his late-race surge. I say how he charged down the home straight, his face twisted in pain, but didn't give up. I'm sure that in those last moments Gallagher felt a crushing numbness in his legs that spread to his entire being, stealing his will. But Gallagher fought through it, proving he could, making me proud. His fierceness surfaced like a budding flower, but was it just a tease?

"Team running. Team running . . . ," I say with conviction. The trio of Dunn-Gallagher-Solebello was only twenty-two seconds apart. And Dunn was only twenty-one seconds behind Silvestri. "If you gain on the guy ahead of you, everyone will run faster," I say to all.

As the boys dress in their sweats for a cool-down jog, I'm sure to touch each boy: an embrace around the shoulders, a pat on the rear, a brush across the head. I feel their sweat. I want this to be personal. We have something at stake together.

I am drawn to a passage in the book *The Wonder of Boys*, by Michael Gurian, a family therapist. He writes, "When we work with boys, we do them and ourselves a great service by opening up to them an equal measure of adventure and mission. Their individual lives must become an adventure in which they discover, experientially, who they are and, in that discovery, get 'hooked up' with their own power. Simultaneously, they must search for the mission or missions which permit boys to fully bond with their fellows . . . and fully discover themselves as spiritual beings who are united with all things."

Boys hide their feelings like the earth hides the sun. Boys communicate through action and nuance. No one will tell me (as a Caitlin or a Marie will tell the St. Rose girls' coach) that he enjoys the team, can't wait to run and, yes, Coach, your point about drinking more water is a fine one, I can see how it's working for me. I must become a detective. The boys reveal themselves in their running, yes; but I'd like more feedback, I'd like a boy, just once, to offer something about how he feels.

Brock's training question is perhaps a start. I'm not that concerned about the workouts. I feel I know all the running options. The issue is whether I am able to engage the boys to feel free enough—to let go of inhibitions—and push to the limit. They are beginning to understand the honor in the struggle.

My mission embraces the question of art versus science in teaching. When I taught school in the seventies, the first year I knew nothing about handling thirty-two teenagers within four walls for forty-five minutes at a time. I taught composition, which I knew something about. I could have been a Ph.D. in literature. No matter. Until I learned to "manage the class" with my particular style of firmness, caring, and humor, no teaching took place.

It's the same with the team. Until I can tickle the boys' souls, excellence will not occur. This tickling cannot be taught. It's who you are. There are coaches who know little about training methods but are geniuses in relating to kids. Some do it with bluster, others with a whisper. A few have both, the art and the science. Joe Newton from Illinois has both. Pat Tyson, a free-spirited coach in Spokane, Washington, has both. I think I know the science; my art is a work in progress.

Departing Lincoln Park, Solebello calls to me, "We did pretty good for St. Rose, don'tcha think, Coach?" *Pretty good for St. Rose?* I cannot fault Solebello. I've heard that sentiment before. "Forget about St. Rose," I say. "The school hasn't won anything in twelve years. How about CBA? Did we do pretty good for CBA?"

Image changes slowly. St. Rose, perhaps like any small parochial school, functions on a certain level of small-mindedness, which is not all bad. The *Asbury Park Press* is the paper of record. Akin to the famous *New Yorker* cartoon, there's the Shore, combining Monmouth and Ocean Counties, and then the rest of the country. But parochialism has not hurt the Roses' baseball, basketball, soccer, and even golf teams, which are among the area's best. School culture looks down on cross-country, however, and the boys get the message. All it takes are derogatory remarks by other kids. Real athletes play ball. The others run.

I try to counteract that thinking, but not by denying its existence. I emphasize our solitariness, our team apart, like a special commando unit, with our own, more demanding core values. If someone complains about a hard workout, I say, hey, no problem, you don't have to run cross-country, go ahead and play soccer and kick a ball around for three hours. They smile. They're glad to hear my rap. I say I'd love to see the soccer team try running at Holmdel Park. They'd *plotz*.

On Monday at practice, the boys look forward to my handouts summarizing team performance. The writer in me provides all the details including a compliment about each boy—like the one for Gallagher: "Very gutty run, rallied for fast finish." I'm honest but gentle with Lavender: "Went out too fast, needs to hold back at start." These flyers and their messages of commitment are a hit with parents and St. Rose administrators.

I also fax the summaries to local sportswriters. The *Press* rightly gives us little coverage. The *Coast Star* practically ignores us once the season starts. The reporter assigned to our team misses some meets and is often a week behind. If he did that with football, he'd be transferred to Guam. No matter. I fuss over the reports, which I will bind into a gift-like book at season's end.

Just when the mood seems properly serious as we prepare for next weekend's trip to North Carolina, Sgt. Pepper, back from the basketball wars, fills the air with a tone all his own. "Hiya, Coach, are we going to have drinks in the limo, because I'd like to place my order now," says John Lennon.

John Leschak's parents have volunteered to hire a limousine to ferry us to the airport. With logistics complicated, I won't be in the limo with the team. That worries me. I start to wonder if the trip is a mistake—will I regret it? But I okay the limo and make sure the school okays it. Brock's dad, Bob, who has spearheaded our fund-raising, will be coming so he'll be the designated adult en route. The limo expresses the Leschaks' appreciation that I've included John, who won't be competing, on the trip. I'd announced that John would be my assistant coach for the weekend. I always wanted an assistant coach with studded jewelry and spiked hair.

"So whaddaya say, Coach, drinks on the limo?" Lennon persists.

"Sure, John, milk it is. Whole or skim for you?"

Lennon's smile lights up a drab day in Belmar. You can't get too angry with a kid that smooth, even if he does play basketball. But his goofing posture continues and he works the team like Shecky Greene works Atlantic City. I pull Lennon aside and tell him point-blank: "This has got to stop. Our trip is important. We have to be focused and at our best in Charlotte. The trip is a reward. Let's not spoil it." He agrees to cool it. I don't threaten him with not being taken on the trip, but it's on my mind.

I take Brock's advice and send the boys on a one-hour run, about eight miles. They ask if they can change direction for once and run north, from Belmar through Avon and Bradley Beach to Ocean Grove, and back. Sure. I'd checked my logs and realized that the boys' summer base work amounted to less mileage than I'd thought. Maybe I was kidding myself. I'd used summer compliance as a carrot for our trip. But that was flimsy leverage. We'd had to book the trip months before.

The boys averaged less than two hundred miles each, a paltry investment. You can't make up for that; what's done is done. The season is here. We have our agenda, another fourteen meets, and we have to get in our speedwork and our hills and take easy-jogging rest days, and there's always a school function like a religious retreat to jar the week. We do what we can.

The boys run the boards and I drive over to Bradley to check on them. With vacationers peeled away, the native population reveals itself and we see Hasidic Jews and black folks along with St. Rose wise guys who streak down Ocean Avenue, their shirts and ties askew, in sports cars after school.

I can't tell whether the school, monk-like amid the beach hedonism, contains students, mitigating their teenage desire to raise hell; or whether the closeted place fosters a seething rebellion waiting to explode. On my team, I see some boys arrive bursting with anarchic energy and others who'd just as soon take a nap.

While the boys run, I nap in my car. That's a first. I've been struggling to help with my father, who's used up his time at a rehab center and moved to a sub-acute-care facility near me. These are nursing homes with a certain number of beds for short-stay rehab patients. Dad continues to receive physical therapy, occupational therapy, and speech therapy. My mother visits every day, and stays all day. In a way, she is a patient, too.

My parents are married fifty-five years. They are a handsome couple, popular in their retirement community for their youthful looks and get-up-and-go attitude. In their wedding picture, with my father in his marine uniform and mother in her flowing white gown, they look like movie stars. My father, even in recent years, has been taken for Cary Grant. My parents' tastes are simple and they'd enjoyed glowing good health, promising blissful years ahead.

So Dad's stroke is taken hard by us all. The therapy never seems good enough, especially for my younger brother Les who, as always, has taken the lead in looking after things. He practically stops working to tend to Mom and Dad. Dad rarely complains. When he lugged soda cases in the snow, he never complained. From what I know of Dad's war experience, which included heavy combat in the South Pacific, he never complained in the foxhole, either.

I have Dad's work ethic but not his endurance. The ordeal weighs on me. Every night I collapse, spent. I have no energy to run. People ask me if I run with the team. Supervise teenage boys—and run? Right now, I swim. That's easy, relaxing, and it helps clear my head.

"Coach! Wake up. Coach, get up . . ." The boys run by and rouse me out of my stupor. I'm a little embarrassed but also feeling it's okay if the boys see evidence of my draining efforts on their behalf. When the run is done, I count the practice, including warm-up and cool-down, as a ten-mile day, our first. The boys have worked up huge thirsts but some—Gallagher, of course; Lennon, of course— have no water bottles. I'm pissed. "You'll die from dehydration," I say. "You'll ruin all the work you put in."

We depart and a few guys traipse down to the 7-Eleven for gargantuan sodas and other junk. The boys have no weight problem. They're beach-thin. Today their running burned up about one thousand calories, but empty foods do nothing for their energy. Diet laxity, as I see it, is symptomatic of the mass-market herding I'm working against. Also, research and plenty of anecdotal evidence have shown that you can be fit but not healthy. You can be in shape to run and compete, but a poor, high-fat, artery-clogging diet can slowly kill you.

As health columnist Jane Brody wrote in *The New York Times*, we are living in a "toxic" food environment. "In it, people from infancy on are continually tempted to eat too much of the wrong foods." The best-selling book *Fast Food Nation*, by Eric Schlosser, states, "A significant number of teenage boys are now drinking five or more cans of soda a day." That, says Schlosser, amounts to fifty teaspoons of sugar. He adds that boys now drink twice as much soda as milk.

I'd like my boys to have it all, fitness and health and a run-for-life attitude. I show them the milk-mustache ads featuring track athletes like Olympic star Michael Johnson. Marginal ammunition against the marketing onslaught of the burger-and-fries industry. Fast food, like so much else in our culture, is disposable. Running has lasting value. You need qualities of lasting value to sustain running. "Everything works together," I tell them. "Be a runner twenty-four hours a day."

Lifelong running will be an issue in Charlotte, because whenever elite teams gather, there are questions about coaching superior athletes for the moment or for the future. Some people feel you can't do both. If you work a kid extremely hard in high school, you risk burning him out. A rap against certain prominent high school coaches is that their runners fare poorly in college. I wish I had to face that problem.

I take what I can from the best coaches and realize I need to do more mental training. All training, of course, has mental elements.

But specific mental training, like visualization—that is, picturing your goals played out—is seen as critical to success. Joe Newton's top cross-country runner from last fall, Don Sage, who went on to run a four-minute mile in his final high school track season, said he psyched himself up by "visualizing the race and focusing on hitting my times." Another top high school runner, Ricky Brookshire of North Carolina, agreed. "I visualize myself running the perfect race over and over again," he said.

The day before our Charlotte departure, after the running is done, I sit the boys down on the boardwalk for visualization. I get them still, have them close their eyes and block out all noise. Not easy with cars roaring by. They giggle at first but then get into it. I tell the boys to imagine their most cherished goals. Keeping up with teammates at practice, conquering the Bowl, scoring high in a race, you pick the moment. Hold that thought, keep it in your mind, see it happen for sixty seconds.

They remain quiet to the end. Opening their eyes, the boys look refreshed. "So, Coach," says Solebello, "does this stuff really work?" Lennon says, "Of course it does, you ass—" but catches himself. He finishes, "Coach knows what he's doing." Thanks, John. I explain how the mind affects the body—indeed, controls the body—and they listen closely. I remind them of a race two years ago in their freshman season—the nosebleed race.

Nick, one of our Fab Freshmen, was a tall, lanky boy with a long, flowing stride. I thought he could be better than Lavender. Nick loved to run. He attended every summer practice and gushed with pride. His parents told me that running was all he talked about. But Nick was also a tragicomic figure who found every way to stumble. In our first meet, he took a wrong turn, losing time. In practice at Holmdel Park, his foot caught a tree root and he went splat on his face. At an away meet on a mountainous course, Nick fell down a hill, twisting his ankle.

Still, he was our number two runner, right behind Lavender, as we ran the freshman division of the Shore Coaches Invitational, a statewide meet, at Holmdel. Half a mile into the 2.1-mile race, as I waited for the boys, Nick came into view and called to me in panic. "Coach . . . Coach, my nose . . ." His bloody hand covered his face. "Coach, my nose is bleeding, what should I do?" I told Nick to "keep on running, you're doing great, don't worry about your nose, it'll stop."

I raced to the next checkpoint, about 1.5 miles. Nick ran by in third place, still close to Ryan, now in second. "Coach, I'm still bleeding. Look, it's all over my uniform." Nick's combination of helplessness and raw strength made for a hilarious scene, and I had to contain my laughter. "Nick, great race, you're third, go after Ryan, you're almost done."

Nick raced home third, on Ryan's heels, and St. Rose won the race in one of the best freshman showings of the entire meet. Crossing the finish, Nick was more concerned about his dirtied uniform than his nose. We cleaned him up and lauded his efforts under duress. I promised him the stains would come out in the wash.

At the next practice, Nick came up to me with a thoughtful expression and said, "Coach, y'know at the meet I was so concerned about my nose I never had time to think about how tired I was."

How did a freshman, and Nick no less, come to such an acute understanding? That day I quickly gathered the boys, reminded them of Nick's heroics, and had Nick repeat what he'd said. I said this was a perfect example of how emotions can affect you. "If you focus on how tired you are, you'll get more tired, slow down, and run poorly. Think of something else and your mind will be free to lift your body" . . . as I put it . . . "to the heavens."

It was a big idea for freshmen to absorb. I thought, *If only the other boys would come down with nosebleeds.*

Nick came down with midseason shin splints and was lost for the rest of the season. He took the injury hard, feeling lost on the sidelines. At the school's fall sports awards banquet, I gave Nick the Most Dedicated Runner Award. When Nick went out for the spring track team, the first-year coach had him run the hurdles on little practice and Nick got injured again. Then he seemed to disappear.

When I heard that Nick might not return for cross-country the next fall, I spoke to his parents. They told me he'd fallen in with the wrong crowd and said he no longer liked running. I was shocked and angry. I could not—would not—believe it. The parents agreed to bring Nick to the beach one Sunday for me to meet with him. I gave it my best shot but failed. Nick wouldn't budge from his new thinking. He insisted he didn't like running—not then, not ever.

Was this the same Nick who glowed after each summer run? The other guys affirmed that Nick was hanging out with neighborhood misfits. Now, concluding the mental training lesson, I tell the boys it'd be great if we still had Nick on the team. They agree. They remember the nosebleed episode like it was yesterday and get the point. Only too well as Lennon says, "Coach, wanna know what I think about in races?" Okay, I'll bite. "Girls, Coach, what else?"

That remark brings talk about the trip to Charlotte and how we'll mingle with teams from all over the country. "You sure there are teams from California, Coach?" says Lennon. Leschak perks up, raising an eyebrow. "Yeah, Coach, California girls, right?"

5

Carolina Mud

The thought of a plane trip with eight teenage boys has me shaking my head as I wait for the limo to arrive at Newark Airport. What surprises am I in for? Do I really need this? In Charlotte, I want to get closer to the boys in a family way, but the need to watch over them twenty-four hours a day is bracing. At practice, when the boys dash blindly across the street to run the boards, I have to physically restrain them as traffic flies by. Will I need a leash in Charlotte?

Years ago at a national high school meet in San Diego, one boy didn't show up at a mandatory dinner for all competitors. Officials were frantic. Was the boy abducted, hurt, up to some mischief? No, he'd just gone out with a friend. The event managers sent the boy home. Ejection is not one of my options.

The boys had practically shamed me into our trip. Michael Dunn said the girls' team traveled, why can't we, Coach? The St. Rose girls' team went to a meet in Florida hosted by Disney. Dunn said, why can't we go to Disney, Coach? I knew the school baseball team had gone to a tournament in Hawaii. Dunn said, why can't we go to Hawaii, Coach?

The limo arrives at Newark on time, but within minutes three boys—Ruhl, Gallagher, and Leschak—disappear in search of a food concession. I think, *Hawaii, are you kidding?* The plane is set to take off and I have to race through the airport to find these characters. When I do, I rip them apart in the open. I tell them, how are you going to have half a chance to run well against national competition in the Great American Cross Country Festival if you can't even be responsible enough to board the flight on time? People munching their airport burgers must think I'm a tyrant.

The rest of the trip is smooth.

I'd given the boys and their parents a three-page, single-spaced memo with every detail and contingency accounted for. Everything from the airline seat assignments to who's rooming with whom at the hotel to the day-by-day itinerary including the time we'll eat breakfast.

To the boys, rooming arrangements are a big deal. I know that the older guys do not want to room with the younger Leschak. I decide to put Leschak in with Lavender. I feel Ryan will be able to take charge of Leschak, keep the reins on him. Ryan, like me, gets a kick out of Leschak's goofy-but-intelligent bent. I find more and more that Ryan and I have a lot in common.

I wonder if Pat Tyson's Mead High team from Spokane, Washington, has to worry about keeping the reins on anyone. I want my boys to meet Pat, meet his athletes. I want them to see that the state-champion Mead Panthers are regular guys like the Running Roses but with a burnished quality that has them seeking freedom—elevation above the ordinary—through the rigors of cross-country. I want the boys to know they can have a barrel of fun this weekend, but that part of the fun is meeting the greats and witnessing how they do it. As I wrote to the boys in my trip memo:

You are being rewarded for your hard work over a period of years with this opportunity to participate in one of the premier high school events in the United States. We raised $3,000 to make the trip possible. This is a privilege. Make the most of it. Run your best. Meet people. Make friends. Learn from what you see. Become a more committed student-athlete, a more committed individual. This is not a 'vacation.' We are going to compete in a challenging race against top-flight competition. That is our main purpose. Running is our mission . . .

Settling in Charlotte, I feel St. Rose is like the obscure Indiana basketball team in the film *Hoosiers* traveling to the big city. Though our boys try to come off as worldly and cool, they shrink in the presence of peers who travel the high school circuit and have the swagger of scholarship athletes. Even Lennon, bossy as ever among our group, is subdued and awestruck amid the other teams.

All our boys are in awe. "These guys are the best in the country," says Lavender. "Even Alan Webb is here." Webb attends South Lakes High in Reston, Virginia. He's considered the best young American mile prospect since Jim Ryun and a potential Olympic medalist. Webb ran close to a four-minute mile last season as a high school junior.

"Yeah, Webb," I say. "He's just like you but, so far, he tries harder." I use whatever leverage I can muster: I tell the boys that Webb started out in sports as a swimmer and in freshman cross-country he was not at the level of Lavender. Lavender smiles. He's smart enough to see through coaching hyperbole.

Webb's presence serves up a number of adolescent development issues encapsulated by the event, which was created a year ago by Rick Hill, a prosperous Charlotte real estate man. Initially, Rick called me to see what I thought about a meet that would invite teams from around the country, based on the "Super 25" national rankings I compiled in my cross-country newsletter. This would be a first for high schools: a national invitational with team championships on the line and expenses paid to select schools. There was already an individual championship, sponsored by Foot Locker, at the end of the season.

When Rick outlined his plans, I thought they were noble but I had reservations. I did the rankings to bring recognition to deserved schools and the sport. When CBA earned a ranking, the *Asbury Park Press* would carry stories for weeks on how high the Colts would go, whether they could even be number one. But inevitably some people took the list too seriously and corrupted it in the way that soccer and Little League have been corrupted.

One coach in Michigan sent me a nasty fax and cancelled his subscription when I changed his team from number one to a tie for number one. Another coach in Utah sent me an e-mail saying he'd gone to great lengths to travel with his team to Great American for one purpose. "I spent $7,000 to get a ranking," said the coach. I e-mailed him back, saying, "If you spent $7,000 to get a ranking, you've got a problem. A ranking is only worth $5,000."

In the rankings game, a sense of humor helps. There was one story that appeared in a Salt Lake City newspaper claiming that a Utah school was demoted in favor of a team from upstate New York because my younger daughter, then in high school, competed for the New York team. Considering that we live about three hundred miles from the school, that would have been some commute.

With the rankings abuzz in Charlotte, my boys ask "if we can be

ranked." I tell them if we win our race, the small-schools championship, I might have to risk the wrath of fellow coaches by ranking
my own team. There are twenty-seven teams from ten states in our
race. One squad, Don Bosco, has come all the way from California.
Don Bosco is composed of Latino kids from a poor area. I remember the widely held view that wanting makes for champions. My
boys work for their keep but they will have cars to drive before
long.

As we turn in for the night, Solebello says, "Really, Coach, how
do you think we'll do?" The top five teams get a trophy, so I
announce that our goal is the top five. Reviewing our opposition, I
know that's a long shot. In addition to Don Bosco, we'll face noted
teams like Cardinal Gibbons of Raleigh and La Salle of
Philadelphia, Marist of Atlanta and Bowman of North Dakota. I
know these teams' coaches and how they operate. Their runners
probably trained five hundred miles over the summer. I worry
whether the Great American meet could knock my boys down so
far they'd struggle to recover.

Or is it really myself I'm worried about? I'm a known figure at
the event and can't help wanting to look good—be considered a
competent coach—among people I respect in running. This is the
high school Oscars, and most of the heavy hitters have turned out.
These are the young athletes who have done exactly what I've
implored my boys to do: care deeply about running as a path to
self-discovery, personal heroism, good citizenship. And these are
the coaches who pave the way.

I sorely need to be part of this world, and here I am, me and my
boys, my five juniors, the two seniors, plus my assistant coach,
Leschak, his gaze blissful, his body jiggly with jewelry, and asking
repeatedly, "So where are the girls, Coach?"

The next morning we practice on the racecourse at McAlpine Park. On the bus provided by the meet, my boys make their first contact with the opposite sex. Setting the tone for the weekend, Lennon and the others freeze with fear while Leschak breaks the ice with aplomb. Leschak approaches any girl, even the prettiest—even seniors—and in minutes they're chatting up a storm while the rest of my team is stunned and speechless. We gain comfort seeing another team from New Jersey, Cherokee, who is rated a chance of beating CBA this season. Cherokee is in the boys' championship division. All racing is at the standard 5K distance.

We find McAlpine Park flooded. It's been raining all week, the remnants of Hurricane Helene. The rain comes and goes but the damage has been done. Park roads are closed. Connecting paths to the course are cut off. Buses can't get through. It's a mess. Rick Hill puts on a good Piedmont face, but the forecast is for more rain and he says city officials are giving him a hard time. For safety reasons, they might have to cancel the meet. No one believes this. I certainly don't. In my four decades of watching cross-country, I can't recall any meet canceled. Rain and miserable conditions are part of the sport. You take pride in it.

The boys jog the course, which is mostly flat. I tag along pointing out strategy. There's a long opening straightaway, and I warn the boys about going out too fast. Midway, there's one small hill, nothing like our Bowl back home, and I say, you're hill runners, this is where you should make your move. We try to skirt the puddles but sink to our ankles. I complain about this but the boys laugh and enjoy it.

We mingle with the boys' team from Long Beach Poly High in California and the girls' team from Campbell County High in Wyoming, both championship contenders. I introduce the boys all the way around. They're wary. They realize this is a society apart. We watch the Campbell team running hard quarter-mile repeats with competition less than twenty-four hours away. The Campbell coach, Orville Hess, records his runners' times on a clipboard sheltered from the rain. Why push now? Hess says he likes to keep his runners' legs moving close to race day. He doesn't worry about tiring them out. The kids are strong from running up to eighty miles a week over the summer. During the season, the Campbell runners come to school at five thirty in the morning to get in a few miles and some weight training before class; then they have their regular practice after school.

The Campbell athletes are humble and respectful and they speak in complete sentences. While my boys ask me if they'll get a chance to go to the local mall, the Campbell runners ask me questions about running and refer to the "oxygen delivery system." I have the boys meet Campbell's star, Alicia Craig, the girls' favorite. I tell them she ran ten miles a day last summer. The boys are impressed but must be wondering: *What are we doing here?*

Craig says her favorite book is the Bible, her favorite food is oatmeal, her favorite movie is *Chariots of Fire*, and she doesn't watch TV. Craig is clearly not among the 48 percent of twelve- to seventeen-year-olds whom the *Today* show says have tried illicit drugs. She's a National Honor Society student who has hiked 14,000-foot peaks in the Rockies and is headed for Stanford and perhaps the United States Olympic Team.

As much as I want Craig's values to be a template for my boys, I see an unhealthy flip side to the overachieving youngsters who lead the way in distance running. There's a high percentage of physical and emotional burnout among girls, in particular, who often excel at thirteen and fourteen before puberty rounds out their lithe frames;

many delay growth with their high-mileage running, which keeps body fat low, stalling adolescent development. A resulting lack of estrogen causes brittle bones, and stress fractures in the legs and pelvic area are epidemic in this group. One thirteen-year study of high school sports that I wrote up for the *Times* showed girls' cross-country first in all sports, ahead of football, in frequency of injury.

That's a number one ranking that should frighten us, but I see little evidence of any collective effort to steer these "twigs," as one coach calls them, onto the right path. We've lost many top girls to eating disorders. Some coaches, my colleagues, drain what they can out of young girls until, finally, weight gain slows them down and they fade away, to be replaced by the next crop of colts. Parents are often co-conspirators, pushing their daughters till they crack. College scholarships worth as much as $150,000 are at stake.

We had a situation in this vein at St. Rose. A diminutive girl who starred in cross-country had a private coach enlisted by her parents. The girl often practiced apart from the team and took on the aura of a prima donna. The school coach objected and threatened to remove the girl from the squad; the principal backed her up. The girls' parents wouldn't budge.

At one point in the episode, the father, who seemed sincere, called me for advice. I think he assumed that I would side with him. I told him the girls' coach was quite competent and that his daughter, who was also a swimmer and had come down with running injuries, would probably be better off if she stuck to swimming.

My suggestion fell on deaf ears. The parents took their case to the New Jersey state athletic group, which ruled in the school's favor. The girl was an excellent student in line for valedictorian. But the parents' response was to take their daughter out of St. Rose and send her to another school.

To be sure, such a posture is still a lot better than having kids sitting around after school eating potato chips and watching TV.

Boys experience different pressures. In America we keep waiting for a men's savior—like the young Alan Webb—to emerge as a candidate to battle the African runners who have dominated distance running for two decades. The problem is, while a Kenyan boy runs naturally in his youth and then trains patiently into his twenties with his soul propelling him, an American boy is as much as captured by a high school and college system that will have him racing week in and week out for years. Then we complain that these young men let us down.

Ironically, on my team, the boys with the most potential, Ryan Lavender and Brock Silvestri, may benefit from the opposite problem—a poor track program. St. Rose has had inadequate coaching during the winter and spring track seasons, which I feel has undercut my efforts. When the boys leave me after cross-country their progress is stunted. But hopefully when they leave high school they'll take fresh legs and unfinished business on to college.

The best system of all is to have a nurturing coach who can work year-round with the boys and pour his or her heart into every phase of their development, on and off the field. As we leave the park and the drizzle turns to a downpour, we come upon Pat Tyson and his Mead Panthers. Pat's the man.

It's bedlam as dozens of squads depart but there are few buses to take us back to the hotel. The St. Rose and Mead boys scamper to a strip mall for shelter. With continuing talk that the meet will be called off, coaches engage in black humor and Pat, who has weathered such conditions before, is in a giddy mood. He pokes his face into the faces of my boys. He jabs them and asks them if they're running hard, making sacrifices, listening to the coach, doing the right thing. My boys' eyes light up but they nod uncon-vincingly. Pat gestures broadly. He knows showmanship grabs kids and has the personality for it. "Train every day," he says. "Every day." At Mead, Pat walks the halls grabbing kids who are too thin for football and too short for basketball and makes them cross-coun-try runners.

Pat learned from the masters. He ran for the University of Oregon, where he was coached by Bill Bowerman and Bill Dellinger. Pat roomed with Steve Prefontaine, the charismatic star who would have been America's greatest runner had his career not been cut short by a fatal car accident in 1975. Pre, as he was called, was twenty-four.

Pre was part of a golden era of American men's distance run-ning, from the early sixties to the early eighties, in which Buddy Edelen, Billy Mills, Bob Schul, Frank Shorter, Bill Rodgers, Alberto Salazar, and Craig Virgin led the world. Then, as though slashed by a guillotine, U.S. success stopped. Shoe companies cut athlete funding. Kids turned to soccer. Computers, malls, and youth marketing enforced immediate gratification. At the same time, running became fully professionalized and the impoverished Africans, seeing riches like candy at races in the United States and throughout the world, took over.

There are still pockets of running excitement, as in Spokane, Washington, where Pat Tyson's energy can fire up the laziest kid. But even Pat can't worry about serving the Olympic movement. He's got all he can handle steering boys away from the mall and onto the cross-country course. That effort we share, and whenever Pat speaks I'm a sponge.

We could use sponges in the unrelenting storm and, all right, I give in, the team heads to the mall for rain gear. We buy slickers and a tent that becomes a team joke. When the boys were freshmen, we saw schools with fancy tents at one meet and I said, if you win your race I'll buy you a tent. They won—but no tent. Until now. I cough up fifty bucks. We laugh about who will be able to set it up. Not me.

Finally back at the hotel, we eye other teams over dinner as Leschak continues his role as social advance man. At one point, the guys stand around like pimply kids at a sixth-grade dance while Leschak rides the elevator meeting girls who don't need makeup to look adorable. Brock's dad, Bob, who's come along for adult support, razzes the boys for their false bravado.

We decide to discuss final race plans in Lavender-and-Leschak's room, the L-and-L suite, as I call it. Indeed, it *is* a suite. Leave it to Leschak to wind up with the best room. We spread out and relax. The boys hurriedly hide stuff I guess I'm not supposed to see. (God knows what that could be.) We kid each other and just talk, and I realize I'm not wearing my coach's hat; that this is the first time I've ever related to the boys as . . . not quite one of the boys, but as a friend.

I defer to them in conversation. Let them feel in charge. Ryan speaks up, saying the tent will keep us dry before running and we should be careful what we eat in the morning, even though our race is scheduled for midday. While Brock leads by example with his perfectly executed races, Ryan leads with a few words and serious tone, as though the point is coming from the coach himself. I think maybe I've been too hard on Ryan. Given his family issues, maybe it's a miracle he's running well at all, never mind threading the needle in race strategy. Suddenly, a top-five trophy seems unimportant.

What seems most important is the communion in the L-and-L suite. These boys *are* my friends in a way—and it's a good thing, too, because I have little faith in the adult world of pretense and dishonor. I can't do anything about that. I can try to resurrect my own self when I see it failing. And I can be a shoulder to the boys, and they to me, as we fashion a trust in the mother lode of simple and soaring endeavors: cross-country running.

The trip has slowed us down, me and my boys. Instead of rushing through daily practice, we sit, talk, wait, eat, talk some more, shop, relate at a proper pace, let impulses and feelings take seed. Someone says, "Coach, did you hear what Gallagher said?" No, what? When I'm told the gaffe, we laugh together. I don't have many men to do that with.

With a measured pace to the day, the boys are more pliable. When I bring up smart training, commitment, a point about next week's critical dual meet against Mater Dei, their focus is resolute. Not everything has to be pinned to the here and now. I remind them about what St. Paul said in First Corinthians 9:24-27 because I know they learned it in school: Run your race by staying focused on your goal.

The scripture reads in part: "Every athlete is in training submits to discipline in order to be crowned with a wreath, which will not last but we do it for the one that will last forever. That is why I run straight for the finish line, why I am like a boxer who does not waste punches. I harden my body with blows and bring it under complete control . . ."

I give Leschak his marching orders for tomorrow: stay glued to me, watch all our gear, make sure the boys have water, be prepared for anything, and don't follow any girls, even those from California, until after the racing is over. Before Leschak answers, I laugh out loud at his gelled, spiked hair, which sticks up like javelins at rest.

"No problem, Coach."

If only we were assured of tomorrow's plan. Rumors fly through the hotel: The meet has been canceled; the meet will be held a day later on Sunday; the meet will be moved to a different park; the meet will be moved to a quarter-mile track and athletes in waves will run the 5K distance around the track; the meet will be changed to a road race and follow a one-mile loop around city streets. I feel for Rick Hill. We watch the weather channel. Is the hurricane gone yet? Pat Tyson holds court in the lobby like *No problem, babe, we're running, we're here, everything's cool, let's rip through the mud.*

On Saturday, I'm up and out before dawn to check the weather. In the darkness, I hear "Good morning, Mr. Bloom." It's Alicia Craig and her Campbell County teammates from Wyoming. They're doing what they always do on the morning of a meet: running three miles before breakfast.

The skies clear but it takes hours to find out if we are racing or not. Finally, the word comes—yes. But the meet will have to start seven hours later, at three o'clock. That's unheard of, but no one balks. We're running! Our eleven fifteen boys' small-schools championship race will now go off around six thirty. By then, the muddy paths should be at their worst; we'll be running through rivers. I start worrying about injuries, twisted ankles. I worry too much but can't help it. Sometimes you have to throw out the coaching manual and let your boys fly.

Meet officials have done their best with the park, but it's too small and drenched and feels like Woodstock without the pot. Thousands of people congregate looking for a dry spot. Music blares, flags fly, balloons are poised for the heavens. Hill won't give up on the carnival atmosphere. He wants the athletes, especially the elites, to be treated like royalty. He feels they deserve it.

We find a tolerable wet spot and stake our claim. Lavender sets up the tent and everyone crawls in to test it. I remind Leschak he's responsible for everything: the tent, the gear, everything. "No problem, Coach." We see other athletes wrapping their shoes in tape to secure their laces in the mud and decide we'll do that, too.

My theme for the day is that this is great, the true runners shine in the toughest conditions. I tell stories about miserable conditions for cross-country, from high school meets that I ran in New York, to one national meet in Wisconsin where my tape recorder froze, to the 1979 world championships in Limerick, Ireland, where John Treacy, an Irishman, won under tremendous pressure and was coated with mud afterward. Treacy, an unassuming athlete, once told me that he got up on the morning of that race and knew he would win it. I remember his words: As his race developed, said Treacy, "I had absolutely no pain."

"But Coach," says Silvestri, "he's a world champion." I say that he was first a teenager like you running in the mud. Then I launch into a spiel about Lynn Jennings, who has won nine U.S. national cross-country titles and three world championships. To Jennings, the worse the conditions, the better she likes it. "Let bad weather work in your favor," she counsels. "Learn to say to yourself, 'I'm a cross-country runner. I can handle it.'"

The high school stars have this mind-set, and you can see it in their countenances and body language as the championship divisions take off. When Alan Webb and Alicia Craig and their teammates line up for the start, they take a series of final warm-up sprints off the line, splashing through the mud with abandon, daring any circumstance to get in their way. I envy their courage and try to get a closer look at their faces as my boys line the sidelines to see the events. The stars all look the same: deep in thought but unafraid.

Craig once told me, "My faith in God is a very important part of my running." Do my boys feel that way? If they did, would they ever say it? I struggle with how to help them affirm the connection. One journalist friend of mine who ran at a Catholic high school told me his coach would often quote scriptures like Philippians 4:13—"I can do all things through Christ who strengthens me."

I sense my boys feel abetted by a higher power. I don't want to come off as preachy, and—being Jewish—my mouth does not easily quote the New Testament with conviction. I try for a more nuanced approach, seeking to fortify some touchstone that we, Jew and Catholic, share. It's about realness, authenticity. It's about living an honest life. Running can teach that.

Craig's race starts and we see how the smart runners find the paths of least resistance. Some stretches are swamp-like; others almost dry. The kids who lag suffer the most as a hundred kicking heels splatter them with gook. Craig finds unexpected company at the front from an undefeated sophomore from Colorado, Megan Kaltenbach, running her first national meet. Like a tutor, Craig lets her opponent stick close for two miles. Craig then pulls away to win by thirty-seven seconds in 17:30. I estimate that the conditions slowed her time by about twenty seconds but, Craig says, "I wasn't concerned about my time."

With her victory taken for granted, Craig is more fixed on her team, given a chance to defeat Saratoga Springs, the favorite from New York. Another lesson for St. Rose: We see girls crossing the finish, their skin barely visible in the mud, not giving an inch, fighting for every place, every second, holding position in the finish chute to make sure no one moves up and gains a single point she did not earn. They gasp for air in the humidity and grab one another's shoulders to stay on their feet as coaches greet them with hugs and water bottles.

Saratoga defeats Campbell, 81-87. Six points is nothing. If one Saratoga girl got complacent for just an instant at any point in the run, she would have lost a few spots and cost the team victory. It would have been a long ride home—Saratoga came by bus. The coaches, Art and Linda Kranick, have no children of their own and consider the girls "our kids." They expect to win. Saratoga has been number one in the country five times, and this victory affirms its ranking this season.

"Glue," I tell the boys. "That's how Saratoga runs. They stick like glue." The boys see how they cross the finish: one Blue Streaks uniform after another in packs. Most of the team members look like little girls. Their wafer-thin bodies disguise toughness. Some join the varsity in seventh or eighth grade; this is permitted in New York State. I think that's bad policy, putting the younger kids through too much.

Saratoga had one girl, Erin Davis, who starred in the eighth grade, then the next year became the only freshman to win the Foot Locker high school title. Davis enjoyed an excellent high school career but fizzled in college. Another Saratoga star, Cheri Goddard, strapping like a swimmer, started excelling in tenth grade, went on to college success at Villanova, and was the top-ranked American 5,000-meter runner in 1999. I feel that a girl who is a prepubescent star risks aborting her future.

Boys can't be stars too soon because the bigger, stronger, more mature juniors and seniors prevail. Boys develop muscle in linear fashion, have fewer early injuries than girls do, and progress from point A to point B predictably. Girls wake up one day with breasts and hips and social awareness, and it's over: Many girls slow down, suffer injuries, or find other interests.

Even Alan Webb, now lining up to race, did not dominate the

scene when he ran a 4:06.94 mile as a sophomore. That time was faster than Jim Ryun, the greatest American miler, ran as a high school soph, but Webb still got beat. Webb does not have Ryun's classic lanky miler's build. At five feet eight and 135 pounds, Webb is compact like Prefontaine but more muscular, like a gymnast. He has Pre's appeal, too. He engages fans who, even now, seek his autograph.

My boys stop their warm-up to watch Webb. He's like Elvis on Ed Sullivan. Webb's race is like a coronation. He somehow seems to fly above the mud; or else he's so far ahead he can pick the drier spots. Seeing Webb's control and grace, my boys and most particularly I are lulled into thinking maybe the mud's not that bad after all. Webb runs fifteen minutes flat to win by seventy-five yards and repeat as Great American champion. Afterward, he shrugs off the conditions and says he just wanted to have fun.

Webb leaves a slew of national-caliber runners almost a minute behind. Cherokee's top runner is fifty-two seconds back. Mead's top runner is forty-eight seconds back. Mead places ninth in the boys' team standings, led by Mountain View of Utah. The Mountain View coach tells me his athletes drink forty-eight ounces of fluid at every practice to stay hydrated. I think how lucky I am if four of my guys have water bottles.

"Did you see that, Coach? Webb put them away," says Brock. "Whaddaya expect, he's a four-minute miler," says Lavender. Webb's run buffets my boys, delivering a reality check. *This* is how strong a young runner can be. Webb intrigues me, too. At what point did he *become* great? He was born with good genes, as we say, but why him—what clicked in Webb that enforced his ascendancy? If only I knew.

"Coach," says Mike Solebello, "do you think Webb can beat the

Kenyans?" Someday, Mike, but what can we learn from Webb? Our race is coming up and the boys continue loosening up. They circle for stretching and I say, did you see how Webb held back then made a big move in the second mile, that's how we should run. The boys nod their heads okay. It's getting late, getting dark and three thousand runners have chewed up the course by now. We're a little punch-drunk from the long weekend. "If I feel good, can I take the lead," says Sgt. Pepper. Lavender steals my line, telling John, good idea if you want to finish dead last.

By accident, Lennon makes a point but I'm too stuck to see it. The boys take the starting line and hand Leschak their sweats. Their trademark blacks socks are pulled high to their knees as mudguards.

We see the Latino youngsters from Don Bosco, black athletes from North Carolina, milk-white faces, and every shade in between. My team needs to mix with this diverse community. St. Rose is almost all white, and at most cross-country meets the fields have few black kids. There's still a long-held stereotype in running that funnels black kids into the sprints.

In a moment the race is off and my heart pounds. This is our chance to show we're a good team worthy of national competition. I wait for the boys at the halfway juncture, the best vantage point. Heavy ground limits my mobility. I feel a rush waiting. There's drama in the anticipation. The field will emerge from wooded trails into the gray light, and there's always the hope—irrational but possible—that my boys will override their limits, enter a new domain, and be up there at the front.

The leaders come forth. Five, ten, twenty athletes race by, their legs kicking up puddles, their jerseys blotchy with mud. I count off forty, fifty runners. No Roses. Finally, Brock appears, then Ryan, then the rest, spread out and struggling. The life drains out of me. More than anything, I'm confused. The boys look like they're trying hard but they're not going anywhere. I call out their names but with no rallying cry.

I sink to rationalization and bargain with myself. The plan, the hope, is crushed. I think we don't really belong here. Maybe the guys got it right all along: Have fun, take it light, meet people, why worry. I think, *Okay, settle for a hard run, the heck with team scores, and get experience in the mud that we can take back home. We have enough on our plate in New Jersey, where next week's dual meet against Mater Dei is a crucial test. But still . . .*

The boys circle a lake for the final loop and finish with odd, disturbed expressions and little of the bent-over exhaustion usually seen in the chute. When the boys run well, I know what to say afterward. Cheers, pats on the back, great jobs, reinforce the good things that happened. It's hard to screw that up. Bad race—that's tough to handle. I want to affirm the boys' efforts but let them know it was not good enough. I want to be firm but gentle. The boys beat me to it.

"We made a mistake, Coach," says Brock, who led the team in sixty-eighth, barely breaking eighteen minutes. "I couldn't make up any ground in the mud. We should have gone out faster to get position. I felt good but couldn't pass anyone. There was mud everywhere so the running path was narrow."

Ryan, eighty-eighth, chimes in with the same assessment. They all held back as I'd instructed. For the first time, they all listened to me! There were almost two hundred runners in the field. I should have realized the boys needed a different, more aggressive strategy. Get out good and protect your position. That's what any smart coach would tell his runners on a course inches deep in mud.

I blew it. We got buried, and I let the boys down. I didn't give the team enough credit. It had not occurred to me that they could muster the fight to start out harder and keep the opposition wedged in the shoe-sucking turf behind. Like athletes, coaches need to adapt. In cross-country, you must assess conditions along with the competition. I let myself down, too.

But even though we place twenty-first among twenty-seven teams, I like what I hear from the boys. They're upset. They feel they could have done much better. They're analytical. They see how they could have used their strength for all it was worth. They teach the coach a lesson. Hopefully, they'll still trust my judgment the next time out. We all learn something we can take back home.

The Don Bosco coach clearly got it right. His boys place five scorers in the top twenty for fifty-nine points and the team victory. Bosco would have placed tenth, just behind Mead, in the championship division. Bosco's coach tells me that in his California district boys' soccer is now in the spring so he has no conflict in the fall. Not only that, but soccer players, many of the school's best athletes, willingly come out for cross-country to get in shape for soccer.

I lament my soccer problem, blaming the conflict for team shortcomings. I'm a candidate for Coach Joe Newton's alibi list of one hundred favorite excuses. The boys, again, show me the way. "That was so cool," says Michael Dunn on the bus back to the hotel. "I was in mud up to my knees." Solebello agrees. "I could hear my shoes soaking it up. Cool." Everyone is into it. They compare their stinking, filthy bodies with pride. Running in the mud is the coolest thing they've done. Leschak says, "Look at me, Coach. Clean," but I suspect Leschak wishes he were in the middle of it.

The boys dress for the post-meet party, a trek to another part of town. Empowered by their efforts, as worthy as those of the winners, they carry themselves like adults. Leschak is still the odd man out but, relieved of his duties, is conferred respect in the social arena. "Coach," says Lennon, "we're following Leschak. He's in charge of the girls."

I send them off on their own with Bob Silvestri to chaperone. While I can't quite let go of my disappointment, I realize the team matured this weekend and showed they can shoulder more of the responsibility for their success. It's not all *me* anymore. I think I can rely on the boys to come through on their own. Maybe I can lead them but without dictating. And they can lead me.

Perhaps, in my dominant role, I've stolen some turf from the boys. Kids like to feel in charge. They need to make some decisions for themselves. Has my tone been tilted all along? In my zest for coherence, have I tried to exercise too much control? Where does proper control end and my freak-out control begin?

In the long season, I need to pace myself better. Two meets done and I'm drained. Every meet can't be most important. That's what I tell the boys, don't I? Strong and smart, right? Don't start out too fast or you'll fade. Conserve energy, come on powerfully at the end when it counts. A race is an apt metaphor for the whole season, and it's taken a run in the mud far from home for my boys to teach me what I've tried to teach them.

We're on new and fertile ground now. My boys and I are forging a holy alliance. All we need is endurance to sustain us. Endurance indeed. St. Paul saw endurance as a life pursuit. The title of a movie about the world's greatest distance runner, Haile Gebrselassie of Ethiopia, is *Endurance*. In the film, Gebrselassie, who has set fifteen world records, says, "You work hard and you love God. If you do not have God to help you, your work is nothing."

Though we may have gotten stuck in the mud, I feel that our

team was blessed in Charlotte. I'm so glad I let Michael Dunn shame me into our adventure. As we return home we face our first dual meet of the season, St. Rose vs. Mater Dei, two Catholic schools set to compete in a race postponed because of Rosh Hashanah.

6

Holmdel Heights

As my boys march into Holmdel Park for our opening conference dual meet against Mater Dei, I know one thing: We must win.
Though I'm hardly a member of the winning-is-everything coaching fraternity, the facts are undeniable: Unless we're able to defeat
Mater Dei, we may as well kiss our season good-bye.

The Running Roses have to produce. I have to produce. The
meets thus far have been preamble. The season that counts starts
now. For the first time in four years of coaching, I feel we can't be
happy with doing our best, whatever that is. I have to assure that
our best prevails.

"We gonna win today?" says Justin Gallagher.

Is that the normally sulking Gallagher speaking without provocation? That's a good sign. But Gallagher's sly grin suggests he
knows something I don't. Or maybe Gallagher welcomes the pressure and can't wait to mix it up in the Holmdel hills with the Mater
Dei boys. Maybe I've been pussyfooting too much, putting too
much weight on the experience, the spiritual, and not enough on
beating the pants off some opponent. I've never marshaled any-

thing close to a killer instinct in my own athletics. In my youth, I was the second baseman who *didn't* want the ball hit in his direction. The boys absorb me, the good with the bad. I can't let this weakness get in the way.

I won't give up on hoping the boys can have it all. I want the spiritual and the fight to merge in a seamless success. But how can I expect to excavate Gallagher's deep-seated-but-so-far-mostly-hidden fierceness if I come off as an uncompetitive pushover broadcasting the desire for the ephemeral runner's high?

Chastened, I think about something the CBA coach Tom Heath told me when I asked him, point-blank, why his runners respond with such drive, like their lives depend on every stride. "It's discipline and fear," he offered.

"Fear of God?" I asked.

"No," he said, "fear of Heath."

Are we going to win today? All I tell Gallagher is, "Run smart and we'll do fine." Which is true. But maybe I should have said something like, *You better run your brains out because we're going murder these guys and if we don't you'll have to hang your head in shame, you follow?*

That's the truth, too. Like St. Rose, Mater Dei is small, coed Catholic school. The Seraphs' coach, Mike Tursi, is like me in many ways. He seems more nurturing than tough, and in fact does not teach at Mater Dei but at a school for special-needs children. Tursi is also one of the few coaches fit enough to join me in running around the course during the race. I respect coaches who run. To me, running would seem like a prerequisite. How can unfit coaches with beer bellies inspire confidence in their athletes?

Another myth. When Tom Heath patrols a race site his gut precedes him. He jokes easily about his nonrunner stoutness, but ask former runners of his about the CBA team and they respond with awe. I wonder, am I the wrong man for the job? Have I got it backward? We go to North Carolina, I tell my kids to hang back and be careful in the mud and we get our asses handed to us.

I greet Tursi with a respectful handshake, and we trade war stories about our teams. Tursi's thick in the middle himself, but the guy manages to beat me up the steepest hill in the back woods whenever we chase after the race field. I swear, it's his killer instinct. Tursi possesses an edge that I don't. He wears a look that says his team has come to play, that the score better go his way or it'll be a long bus ride back to Monmouth Junction.

Apparently, Tursi conveys this attitude to his boys. Mater Dei's top runner, Tom Santifort, would sooner swim with sharks than give an inch on the racecourse. Santifort, who cuts an odd figure with a long, thick neck above his slight body, draws every gram of strength from his modest talent. He loves to lead, even to his detriment. Tursi says it's the only way Santifort can run and leaves him be. In this regard, Santifort's even more stubborn than Lavender, who at least has a certain grace in his risky approach. Santifort's a bull. It's as though he feels that anything less than blasting headdown from the gun will disclose weakness, a signal to himself that he cannot measure up.

Last year, when we raced Mater Dei on our home course, I begged our guys to let Santifort have the lead. I didn't want the boys to get big heads at home. They listened. Santifort charged ahead and faded; Lavender took over and won by twelve seconds as Silvestri rallied for a solid fourth. Bingo! But Mater Dei had more depth and defeated us by three points.

That victory propelled Mater Dei to win the conference dualmeet title, and the school went on to capture the 1999 state championship in our division. The Mater Dei boys hoisted Tursi and carried him in jubilation as he waved the first-place trophy aloft. We placed third, sixteen points behind. Even with our young, mostly sophomore squad, we were capable of winning. We ended our season with an empty feeling.

Though Santifort's back for his junior season, Mater Dei has less depth this fall while St. Rose, as everyone at Holmdel Park is well aware, is much better with our scoring unit intact.

With the season a month old, Brock has moved ahead of Ryan as our top runner. I gently pit Ryan against Brock by telling them to stick together. Should I be more forceful, ordering "run together or heads will roll," for a more Heath-like effect? I figure that could mess with Ryan's fragile psyche at a time when he's got all he can handle at home.

The excitement of the day—brilliant sunshine and a sense of destiny we feel as the superior squad—is rattled by the appearance of both Dennis and Karen Lavender, separately, and each accompanied by a new mate. They take their places apart on the field's expanse. It's easy for them to melt into the crowd with several meets running concurrently and parents everywhere, but the Lavender couples are all I see. That and Ryan's face tightening—the last thing we need. Let's not give the boy a ready excuse for a lousy race. *Why can't the opposite happen,* I think. *Why can't Ryan use his problem to deliver a supreme effort?*

Runners do it. Adam Goucher of Colorado overcame his parents' divorce to win the Foot Locker high school championship and become an Olympian and the best 5,000-meter runner in the United States. Anguished by the split, Goucher strived hard, developing a lust for competition that he expressed to me when I visited him in Boulder. "I love controlling a race, chewing up an opponent," he said. "It's raw, animalistic, with no one to rely on but yourself. There's no better feeling than that."

Children of divorce learn to rely on themselves as the ground shifts under their feet. Running, therapists tell me, could give Ryan a sense of control; it is perhaps the one thing he can control now. "Running," says one expert, "can be tremendous therapy when everything else is falling apart."

I think Ryan understands this and sense his use of running as a refuge from the turmoil engulfing him. At practice, though Ryan's worldliness puts him above some of the trite male small talk, he readily chatters away, looking to bond and feel like a regular guy in our team family. Ryan's need for some control may also explain his tendency to set his own rules with a fast pace. With a team to coach, and a victory to chalk up against the defending state champion, I can manage only so much hand-holding.

But inevitably I'm drawn to Ryan, who avoids eye contact with Mom and Dad and seems subdued by the in-your-face appearance, out in the open, of his new and threatening family alignment. Ryan's sanctuary has been violated. Holmdel Park is sacred ground. The park brochure rings true with a quote from the poet Maya Angelou: "Each of us needs to withdraw from the cares which will not withdraw from us."

Who knows that better than I do? This setting is supposed to be my own escape: from the stress of my father's stroke and the need to navigate greater family closeness. Slowly, brick by brick, I become more accepting of family-of-origin intimacy, even looking to it to help fill the void left by my daughters. After practice, when I visit my father at the rehab facility, I kiss his forehead, hold his hand, and counsel my mother on getting through the ordeal. Amazingly, my father's a rock.

Shaken whenever I leave him, I realize I ask more of Lavender than of myself. At odd times, I blow up in tears or lean heavily on my wife for support. Ryan's a rock, too. Who can he turn to? I see how, perhaps seething within, he holds his emotions; how he talks sweetly about his kid sister like, *No worry, she'll be okay.* Yet, I'll kick the sand when Ryan's race is imperfect. He's too good a runner to fall short. I can't let Ryan fail. Reflexively, I bring the mezuzah around my neck to my lips on Ryan's behalf.

Holmdel fills in the late afternoon as athletes crisscross the turf doing their warm-ups. I send the St. Rose boys on their way. Tursi does the same. The weekly card of dual meets with schools from all over the county is a festival of running. Reporters and photographers turn out and fathers leave work early and come with their ties loosened and conference officials in umpire-style garb run the show with serious precision. People congratulate me on how the team is progressing as though our victory is assured. Everyone will scour the results in the next day's *Press*, which lists the top ten runners from every dual meet along with a battery of stats, sidelights, and divisional standings. In running circles, these accounts take on biblical importance.

The boys finish jogging and form a circle for stretching. They talk about teachers and girls and the rain in North Carolina. Michael Dunn, recalling that I presided over the coaches' clinic in Charlotte, says, "Mr. Bloom, we didn't know who you were. How come you want to coach *us?*" Am I still up against a small-school inferiority complex? I'd never mentioned my running background to the boys. I knew you couldn't win teenage hearts with a résumé. I have an answer for Dunn. "Because . . . I love you guys."

Then, somewhat embarrassed, I walk away. I feel it's best for them to contemplate what I've said without me standing there. I suspect that, boys being boys, a remark like that from the coach will be absorbed without comment.

Moments later, from out of left field, Brock brings up last year's unfortunate incident involving Mater Dei. We had a late-season meet against Point Beach at its home course, Ocean County Park, in Lakewood. So did Mater Dei. Our three teams ran together, but St. Rose and Mater Dei were competing only against Point Beach, not each other. Still, I told the boys to use Mater Dei for motivation. We were outrunning the Seraphs when, in the last mile, a number of Mater Dei boys cut the course, which was not very well marked. Tursi was defensive about the action. Mater Dei beat Point Beach handily, so the results stood. But my boys were outraged when suddenly the Mater Dei runners were positioned ahead of them in the final yards. When they complained to me, my reaction was: "Next time, run harder."

I have much the same reaction now. "Don't let it be close," I tell Brock. He takes my command to heart. At least I'm here to keep an eye on Mater Dei, thanks to the St. Rose athletic director, Dick Alger, who each season receives a summer call from me about meet conflicts with Jewish holy days. At first, I was reluctant to ask. I could picture Dick appealing to the A.D. of another Catholic school to change a meet for a Jewish holiday. What political capital did he have to use up for that one? But now it's old hat.

As a lesson to the team, I'd considered letting the original date stand and asking another coach, or even a team parent, to cover for me. I wanted to tell the boys how, when I was their age, I was proud that Sandy Koufax would not pitch a World Series game on Yom Kippur. And also how the observant Christian Eric Liddell, the 1924 Olympic 400-meter champion from Scotland, switched from the 100 to avoid running on a Sunday in Paris.

I want it both ways: to observe my Jewish faith and coach my Catholic team. I fall on the precedent of inclusion set almost a century ago by Abel Kiviat, perhaps the greatest Jewish middle-distance runner ever. A New Yorker from Staten Island, Kiviat set three world records in the 1,500 meters and captured the 1912 Olympic silver medal in that event. Kiviat's family fled the pogroms of Russia to come to America, but as a young athlete Kiviat had few options for support and joined the Irish-American Athletic Club. Kiviat even marched with his teammates in the St. Patrick's Day parade.

The boys know nothing of such running history, so I'm flabbergasted one day at practice when Sgt. Pepper utters the name "George Young." I say, "George Young, the Olympic runner?" Lennon nods. This can't be. Though Young was a four-time Olympian from the sixties and seventies in the steeplechase and 5,000 meters, he remains a rather obscure figure. Lennon wouldn't know Marion Jones from Marian Anderson. How the heck would he know George Young?

"The Prefontaine movie," he says.

I let out a good laugh. Young plays a small role as an opponent of Steve Prefontaine's in the movie, which the boys bring to our pasta party every year on the eve of the state meet. They bring the film not so much to appreciate Pre's guts on the track as for the implicit sexual scenes. Apparently, Pre's sexual prowess was noteworthy, too.

That's okay. Maybe something of Pre's running will rub off on Lennon. But at Holmdel I find out it's too late for that. Lennon's dad informs me his son is quitting the team after the Mater Dei meet. He's got to put all his energy into basketball.

You win some, you lose some. This is a big loss but not unexpected. Now it's official: The team has no margin for error. After the five junior scorers, the soph Leschak and the senior Ruhl are too far behind. One key injury at the wrong time and it'll take a miracle for St. Rose to be a state contender.

As the boys put on their spikes, I tell them that this race is our first big step toward the state meet. They're calm, I'm jittery. I remind them of the self-sufficiency they showed in North Carolina, how they're ready to take more responsibility for their success. "You can't rely on me to push you, you have to push yourselves." I say how fresh we should feel, how we didn't get to race full-out down south because of the mud. Coach's mistake, I admit, again, hoping my humility will fire them up. "Show me—show yourselves—you can do better."

And then, as the last laces are tied, Dennis Lavender and Karen Lavender suddenly exchange coarse words out loud, in the open, daggers flying. The argument seems to involve some matter with Ryan. Emotions heat up and Karen's boyfriend takes a threatening step toward Dennis. Just when I think I may have to intervene to prevent blows, the parties simmer down.

Every eye turns to Ryan, who would crawl into a woodchuck's hole if he could. Ryan looks away. The other guys look embarrassed for Ryan; they're stunned and fearful, as though witnessing a teacher-student confrontation at school when it's least expected. Ryan allows a crooked smile of resignation, like, *You know my situation, that's just the way it is right now, I'll deal with it.*

I give Ryan his space. I don't want anyone to think he's weak and needy with a race to run, or that he's too downtrodden to handle things by himself. My sober expression says, *Yeah, we'll get through this, Ryan, the team, all of us, so let's get ready to run.* I plan to speak with Ryan alone when I can.

The two teams are called to the start. Tursi and I offer our last instructions, then we both run hard up the long, opening ascent to wait for the field in the hills. After a couple of minutes, we're both breathing hard and stop on the dime. Our partnership is a little awkward. We will follow the same path, shouting much the same messages of running smart and strong and pushing past pain, but we are also antagonists, rooting silently for the other guy's team to falter. If it's close, like last year when the teams were virtually tied until the final strides, we will scream ourselves hoarse in desperation, practically drowning each other out.

Couple of high school cross-country coaches doing their jobs on a Tuesday afternoon. Tursi, like most coaches, handles the team for all three seasons—winter and spring track in addition to cross-country. He can maintain continuity with his athletes and is always around to draw kids out for the team. St. Rose asked me to do the same and I would do it if I had the time. Being a one-season coach has hurt my recruiting and it has also given Dick Alger problems finding a capable track coach.

The current St. Rose track coach is a black man whom I wish I could work with but can't. I'm glad he's black because St. Rose has no black staff and the boys need a black authority figure. The coach takes a tough-love, drill-sergeant approach that the boys seem to like. He comes off as streetwise and cool, appealing to suburban white kids. He insists on calling me "Mr. Bloom," and with a certain attitude, which I take as condescending.

But my issue with the man is that his coaching background is in age-group track, in which young kids are trained far too seriously in pursuit of records and trophies. A year ago, he tried to enlist my team in his summer program. That would have meant more competition at a time when they needed base training and a rest from racing. Some of the boys and their parents were temporarily drawn to the coach's promise of victories. I was furious. Fortunately, the boys ended up sticking with me.

After about 1:45 on the watch, Santifort powers up the first hill in the lead. With his large head and quick arm movement, he reminds me of a fish. Brock and Ryan follow by a stride. "That's it. Perfect," I call out. Tursi shouts his rap, and he comes off as more warlike in setting his boys against mine. I'm careful not to refer to Mater Dei or Santifort by name or to suggest anything negative about their efforts. It's all about us.

Dunn, Solebello, and Gallagher run by in close order. "Attaway, attaway. Stick together. This is your day." I can tell in the first couple of minutes who's going to run well. A boy's face gives him away. I watch for peace and control, how a boy sticks with the field and shows he's part of the race. Dunn and Solebello are in the game. Hearing my voice, Dunn almost cracks a smile. But he has a way of bouncing, wasting energy as his head bobs and body tilts. "Straight, Mike, straight." He knows what I mean. Solebello shows courage in Dunn's shadow. "Stick together," I repeat while running to the next checkpoint.

As I race after Tursi, who's already left for the shortcut to the halfway point, I notice Gallagher falling behind, his look fearful. I keep thinking that one day Gallagher's going to wake up and lead the team. Especially now that he's informed me he's been running in the mornings before school. This development is a bigger shock than John Lennon knowing George Young.

"At six forty-five," Gallagher announced the other day. "4.8 miles." I don't believe him. After he convinces me, he says he might try to do that every day. Though I caution Gallagher against overdoing it, I feel as triumphant as Sidney Poitier teaching the nuns in *Lilies of the Field.*

So why is the newly ambitious Gallagher lagging today? Partly, it's just Gallagher. I cannot decipher his sullen moods. Gallagher has two sisters, one who is disabled and confined to a wheelchair. He doesn't speak about her except when he can't get a ride somewhere because someone has to be home to watch his sister. After the race, Gallagher tells me he was slowed by stomach distress. Knowing what he eats, I believe him.

The shortcut is a steep, treacherous downhill leading to the Bowl. Hurry down in a rush and you might catch your toe on a tree root and go flying. I step down as though on hot coals and finally join Tursi, and together, waiting for the boys, we pace the bottom of the circular field that gives the Bowl its name.

In many parts of the country and even some sections of New Jersey, dual meets are not a cross-country requirement. There's more than enough invitational competition, and coaches object to a proliferation of meets. If you're always competing, it's hard to fit in enough good practices, and more meets mean increased risk of injury.

However, the Shore Conference requires dual meets, consistent with competition in other sports, which have individual games for baseball or lacrosse along with tournaments and championships. The conference is divided into six smaller conferences based on enrollment and proximity, and St. Rose is in Class B Central along with Point Beach, Keansburg, Henry Hudson, Shore Regional, Keyport, Rumson-Fair Haven, and of course Mater Dei.

While a school like CBA can regard dual meets as a nuisance and collect victories with its third string, at St. Rose the contests give us valuable experience and a chance to win something. The small fields pitting one team against another offer the essence of running: athletes dueling shoulder to shoulder, feeling the spraying sweat of a competitor, pushing through the natural landscape of brush and hills to the waiting finish where every point will count and everyone will know how you did.

And especially at Holmdel Park, where the Bowl strips you bare and you are exposed for the athlete you are as you flash out of the woods like a prophet delivering the truth for the kick to the line. Will the score be 27-28 for your team? Only if you run down the opponent a few strides ahead of you in the last hundred meters. Will the guy charging from behind nail you at the finish? Then, if it's close, the score could be 27-28 for the other team.

That's what many dual meets come down to: who's willing to push harder for one point. Last year, Mater Dei beat us, 26-29. If the Seraphs' second man after Santifort had been content to give up on the home straight (frankly, as a couple of my guys were content to), St. Rose would have triumphed, 27-28. Invitationals and state meets can turn on a single point, too, but in a dense field of 150 or 200 runners you may not have the chance to stare a key opponent in the face and challenge yourself to overtake him.

In dual meets, I can better isolate a boy and coach him during the race. As the field appears on the ridge and heads toward Tursi and me at the base of the Bowl, I hope I don't need to rigorously sway anyone in midrace. It shouldn't be that close. The boys are maturing, each in his own way. They know we're the better team. They're gaining strength. At practice, after North Carolina, they looked forward to their Holmdel debut.

Holmdel Park, a well-kept 347-acre site where families picnic and retirees fish for trout, offers a prize course, the best I've seen. I favor natural courses in which the trails are set from existing pathways as opposed to golf courses or high school grounds that are fashioned into cross-country layouts. Holmdel's a natural. It has everything: challenging hills, quick turns, surface changes from dirt to grass, flat sections for reprieve, tricky downhills, and a lengthy home straight for the sprint to the finish. Holmdel has narrow, wooded trails and broad, open fields. It gives you shade and sun. It protects you from the wind and, within seconds, throws the wind in your face.

Holmdel's formidable route makes it at least thirty seconds slower than most other 5K courses. Jersey teams like CBA often include meets with flat courses on their schedules to build egos and make sure that yours truly, the rankingsmeister, sees how fast they can run. A boy running 17:15 at Holmdel would hit around 16:40 in Charlotte, assuming it was dry.

The same boy would probably run close to sixteen minutes even in your mostly flat neighborhood 5K Turkey Trot. Running the roads is a breeze compared to cross-country. Hills aside, on the roads your shoes grip the concrete and you can maintain a consistent, fluid stride pattern. Heavy cross-country surfaces, often ungroomed, suck your legs' energy. Each stride requires extra effort and a change of rhythm. It's the difference between skiing a manicured trail and going off-piste, the difference between a walk around the block and a hike in the wilderness.

For its wildness, I prefer cross-country to track, which is civilized and predictable and which sometimes favors pure speed over guts. I like what Thoreau said: "Life consists with wildness. The most alive is the wildest."

Run Holmdel's trails and you feel alive. Your senses become acute. Breathing hard from the opening hill, you pick up the fragrant beech and hickory, notice every rock and rabbit, whiff what horses leave behind. You feel your body fly on an undulating section, ache on the Bowl. You get lost in a blissful freedom, overcome by the land's "tranquilizing, sanative influences," as Emerson put it. You reach the finish in reward: an affirmation of character, a denial of age, the culmination of art.

Racing the wilds adds the dimension of strategy. For the young athletes, each Holmdel section requires a different tactic—a burst of power or measured pace, a hard swing around a turn, an elbowed protection of a ribbon of turf, or drafting off a taller boy in the open. There are seven distinct sections, and you run each as a task in itself, joining them like patterns on a quilt.

I counsel the boys on getting position on the opening hill, a gradual ascent punctuated by a short, steep pitch. After the hill come rolling, wooded trails where a smart runner can move ahead despite the congestion; then the long dirt and cinder pathways setting up the Bowl; the pivotal, jarring climb; the flat grounds leading to the tennis courts where it's easy to lose focus; the shaded, seductive downhills taking you back through the woods; and the final home sprint in the sunlight to cheering crowds.

Many a race is won, or lost, on the Bowl. If you fear it, you're cooked. "This hill is your friend," I call to the boys when we practice there. Even Gallagher smiles at that one. When I run part of the Bowl with the team, keeping up with the slower guys and yelling, "You guys are sixteen and can't outrun someone more than three times your age!" I get more smiles. And the boys hunker down and work harder.

Up the Bowl, Santifort is still first and he's got a few yards on Brock, running second, with Ryan moving listlessly in third. Mater Dei has the fourth spot but then Dunn, Solebello, and Gallagher follow and Lennon's our next guy not that far back. If the positions hold, St. Rose will win convincingly. Despite Tursi's urging, Mater Dei's second group has little fight, and as the boys pass Tursi hangs his head seeing imminent defeat.

Then Tursi and I face our own Bowl—the climb back up the steep, rutted shortcut to a clearing at the tennis courts a little past two miles. I can barely make it all the way without walking. The boys chug by with positions unchanged. No one fashioned a big move on the Bowl. I think my boys could tell we had it won, and Mater Dei knew it, too. They all let up like a train slowing down. Except for Santifort. While his legs deaden, he pushes, his stride a stutter step. His face reddens and his small arms jut out like gills. Brock has all but given up in second, and Ryan is in his own world in third. Santifort's going to win the race, and I admire his toughness.

This section near the tennis courts is the easiest part of the course, and the hardest to bear down on because it lacks definition. It's flat. There's a mile left. With the bump-and-grind downhills around the corner and the need to assure you have something left for the finish, this stretch is the one place where a runner thinks he can coast without consequence. It's too far out for a kick, and you've already fried your cookies on the Bowl. You're proud to get this far on your feet and no matter how hard coaches cry for more, you seek a tenuous relief, as your oxygen supply wears thin and your teenage heart pumps 205 beats per minute.

This is where guts and biochemistry meet. The chemistry has been figured out. Guts are another story.

By training hundreds of miles for months on end, my boys' heart muscles have gotten stronger and their hearts' chambers have been stretched. Their blood volume has increased while the blood has thinned, providing more fluid to facilitate sweating, critical in the dissipation of heat that builds up at race pace. After two miles, their hearts pump as much as twenty liters of blood per minute as compared with about five liters per minute at rest.

With more blood at work and moving at a faster rate, plus an increase in red cells, sufficient oxygen is acquired from the lungs and delivered to the active muscles, like the hamstrings and quadriceps that propel the legs. Well, the oxygen supply is never really sufficient. There are always limits. As muscles burn energy, they fatigue, producing waste products like lactic acid. It's a war: lactic acid vs. your fitness level. Lactic acid almost always wins. Sooner or later, my boys' leg muscles are going to seriously fatigue and the quadriceps, the big, hulking muscles in the front of the upper leg, will burn with the accumulation of lactic acid. Your pace slows— what coaches call "tying up."

When I see my boys struggle on the path around the tennis courts, I know what they're going through. A voice from within— a voice heard from the opening strides and now worn thin—allows them to ease up because the pain is great. Ryan grinds his teeth. Mike Dunn's head tilts. Brock's eyes tighten. Mike Solebello's face shows biblical anguish. I almost feel guilty ordering them to "work, work, work . . ."

It doesn't help that the boys led inactive childhoods, watching too much TV, sitting at the computer, being driven everywhere instead of walking. They started running in their teens with weak muscles and thin bones. In a way, it's amazing how far they've come.

Sports psychologists talk about running through pain to a higher consciousness, and I believe in that. Conquering pain in a race combines courage with faith, and we have to count on prayer to work some magic. As St. Ignatious Loyola wrote, "Pray as if everything depended on God, and work as if everything depended on man."

Now, as the boys head for the finish in the throes of pain, they have three minutes of running to go and guts take over. It's like the end of a marathon when you have nothing left. Some runners cave; others find will. Just who will summon the strength, the grace, to succeed is a mystery. I kind of prefer it that way. I like having this one secret, this buried treasure in the mind-body mix of running transcendence.

Tursi and I run the car road to the finish shouting our last, desperate calls. I can see the boys flash through the trees lining the sloping dirt paths. Dunn looks revitalized, sticking with Mater Dei's second man all the way. Solebello's right behind, running his best race yet, his countenance at ease. They've found the will, the guts. Why them? Maybe it's upbringing. Dunn's parents operate with quiet firmness. The boy may have a lazy streak, but his grades put him at the top of his class. Maybe it's too much for him to study hard and run hard—*every day*. Today, Dunn's a runner. Solebello does heavy lifting with his father's construction crew. Physical labor is nothing new to him.

I feel a kinship with Solebello since many of my values were shaped by working with my father. In the summer, he'd wake me at five thirty and we'd take our rumbling '54 Pontiac through Brooklyn to the soda plant in gritty Bushwick, where the product was made, bottled, and loaded overnight onto Dad's truck. I can still smell the dense summer air on that street and the hops from the beer company nearby.

Delivering cases of bottled soda to groceries in run-down neighborhoods was dirty, backbreaking work. I accepted the family responsibility to help Dad during school vacations. We worked in summer heat that could crack the bottles open and winter storms that could freeze them solid. I felt close to Dad sitting next to him in the cab of his truck, watching him plan his route and seeing his biceps bulge as he muscled the heavy soda crates. At night, my mother and I took turns rubbing Bengay into Dad's sore back. Dad's stroke has returned to me that intimate impulse.

Handling the heavy soda cases with Dad made me different in a grown-up sort of way. I learned you had to work for anything you wanted and came to view work and life as one and the same. I never managed to apply the callusing to my own running and instead felt compelled to pass on the values to others, including my daughters as they came of age.

When Allison, my older daughter, ran cross-country, she showed more guts than I could fathom. She ran despite severe breathing problems caused by a bout with exercise-induced asthma. A scorer on a top-ranked Marlboro squad, Allison persevered despite constricted airways, falling into my arms at the finish as I fought back tears. I developed a soft spot for female runners and even now get emotional when I see girls collapse across the finish in agony.

Boys, no matter how whipped, tend to finish tall, trying to sustain their ordained macho postures to the end. Past the finish chute, girls often fall flat on the ground, writhing in pain and perhaps with some confusion as to why their well-trained bodies feel crushed by fatigue. An exercise physiologist, Russ Pate of the University of South Carolina, an Olympic Trials marathoner, told me that after puberty boys have an increase in hemoglobin concentration in the blood—the oxygen-carrying red blood cells. The boost is associated with an increase in testosterone, which girls do not share.

At the finish, meet officials at Holmdel separate boys from girls with a rope. Boys to the right, girls to the left. Santifort trucks it home with his head up and a clean face in 17:48. I make a point of congratulating him. My five juniors—Brock (second), Ryan (third), Mike Dunn (fifth), Mike Solebello (sixth), and Justin (seventh)—hold their ground all the way and St. Rose triumphs with room to spare, 23-34.

Brock's time is 18:00, nowhere near his potential, but the season is young. Ryan's time is a tepid 18:25 but considering the issues on his plate I have no complaints. I'm encouraged by Solebello's best by thirty seconds and by our trailers, Ruhl and Leschak, who also ran their fastest times. This is a decent first shot at Holmdel, where the hills can seem like mountains in late September. We've come through as a team under pressure. But our five-man average of 18:36 will have to improve at least forty seconds by November.

When Tursi tells me it's settled, we're the team to beat for the state title, I'm buoyed; but I still wonder if our collective will is thin and whether my message of sacrifice leading to exaltation is on shaky ground. I can't be any tougher. My words have to work.

My efforts are affirmed by spiritual leaders whom I consult for guidance. Father Thomas J. Paprocki, formerly the chancellor of the Archdiocese of Chicago and a marathon runner, tells me that he recites the rosary while training and that prayer becomes a mantra taking his mind off his body's fatigue. In running, if you take your mind off fatigue, you'll feel less tired. Sports psychologists call this disassociating. Studies have found that elite runners do better with the opposite approach—by focusing on their body sensations to monitor pace and stride.

In high school, my cross-country coach, who on cold days sat in his car smoking a cigar while we ran, told us to think about sex or pickles to rid our minds of the pain. At least he was on the right track. Perhaps I need to broaden the role of prayer with the boys. Paprocki referred me to an article he wrote on the spiritual qualities of running.

"In the Christian tradition," Paprocki wrote, "we speak of sharing our pain with the sufferings of others. When we do so, we quickly become mindful that the soreness of our run-fatigued limbs pales in comparison to the much greater pain of those who are suffering physically from a terminal illness or who are experiencing mental anguish because of the death of a loved one. When I realize this, suddenly my complaints seem trivial and my feet feel lighter."

I express a similar sentiment to the boys each season when I miss practice for Yom Kippur. To emphasize the idea of sacrifice, I tell them it's a day of fasting and someone always asks why. I explain what the rabbi says to the congregation: that you learn what it means to be hungry and draw a kinship, however brief, with the needy. Fasting is also an act of purification. This humbling experience, absorbed in the context of the holy day, a day of awe and penitence and contemplation, a day of pleading prayer that connects the generations, can open the door to the other side, the side of purity. It's the same door I beseech the boys to open when they run and get to the point of pain.

Somehow, everything about you collects in one place like a ledger from above when you face the denouement of pain in a race. You leave your fingerprints on the Bowl. It *is* a religious experience. "Stick with it," I tell the boys. "Open the door." I try to keep it simple. I don't want my language to come off as priestly, and I feel that in the end my persistence will count more than vocabulary. I just know my boys can get through the "doorway," a term also used by Ted Falcon, a progressive rabbi and psychotherapist in Seattle.

Rabbi Falcon describes the other side of a runner's pain as a transcendent place where you reach level upon level of spiritual growth, becoming, in effect, a different person with a different reality. This is the place where we all belong. Falcon says it's a place where you feel the "interconnectedness of all things," as my Rabbi Schechter says, a place where I know deep down my boys want to be. I see how they're growing more comfortable with their evolving consciousness. I see the pride they take in their efforts, how they dismiss boys at school who mess around aimlessly, how they no longer feel alienated as runners but distinct.

Falcon emphasizes that alienation leads us astray. We have to feel connected. And I know what he means because alienation once brought me great peril. The next day I'm reminded of my personal confrontation with the devil when Ryan Lavender, following the family episode at Holmdel, doesn't show up at practice. The other boys say he wasn't in school. As the team proceeds with the warm-up, I call Ryan's house—any boy not at practice without a prior excuse gets an immediate call—and just as the phone rings Ryan shows up at the lake on his bike.

I play dumb and say, "What's going on?"

Ryan says he had to take care of things, that he needed a break. I press for more and finally he says, "I had to take a mental-health day," adding that he ran on his own. I tell him I'll send the boys on their workout and we'll sit and talk. He shrugs okay.

Before 1994, I would not have known what a mental-health day was. I looked at life in concrete terms, did not see the gray areas, never connected the mind and body, dwelled on my work, was obsessed with my exercise, had few friends, tuned out the rest of the world, and existed in some stupid, naive bliss. I drove myself into emotional estrangement.

A deepening, misunderstood alienation resulted in back pain that forced me to stop running for more than a year. The alienation had its roots in my youth when I had little patience for the mundane, kept things to myself, and was indoctrinated with a certain

Jewish superiority in a sea of Christians. The goys were another breed entirely, and deserving of our disdain. The same flight from life's burdens that led me to running also led me to strike out on my own emotionally—to feel apart from almost everyone and everything. Finally, the aloneness consumed me and I was lost.

When the back pain struck, I didn't realize I had an emotional problem. I assumed the pain came from running. No doctor or therapy was able to ease the pain, and I spiraled into depression. I took too many painkillers, got panic attacks, and further withdrew. Getting through each day was a challenge.

This went on for months. I drove my wife to her wit's end, and she had enough on her head with her own ailing mother. During this time I lost a close friend to cancer. The same week my mother-in-law died. My wife's stress over her loss offered the first glimpse of the true source of my pain. She developed a breathing problem. We trekked to doctors and she checked out fine. It was all stress. I was so intent on my wife's situation that during one week when I ignored my back pain it virtually disappeared.

However, my pain eventually returned and as a last resort I saw a physician known for his unorthodox treatment of back pain. He said it was all emotional, that anxiety and anger caused certain people—and I fit the personality type to a T—to develop back pain. The mind gives you a physical pain, which, in the subconscious, you really want because it takes your mind off the more dreaded emotional issues you face. If you ignore the pain, it has no reason to exist and gradually goes away. In time, I came to acutely understand this syndrome and eventually, with the help of a psychologist, the pain went away for good. I was a free man.

Not only was I free but now possessed of a higher consciousness, a recognition of the mind and one's recuperative powers, a sensitivity to the gray areas that can tilt you a few degrees off-center. My mid-youth crisis, as I called it, is one reason I got into coaching. With my daughters out of the house, I needed the sweetness of youth to keep me level; a child's smile always meant that much.

I feel I can apply my greater understanding to the team and when I sit with Ryan at least I can appreciate some of what has imperiled his running. He's gone from being cared for by two parents to a source of conflict in the family. He feels neglected and has to function like a parent himself. He's too proud to pour out his feelings. He's out of sync, steeped in alienation.

It's a clear day and the breeze off the ocean is comforting. We sit on a bench at the lake. Ryan finally opens up. He describes his parents' situation and the disputes that center on him and his sister. He speaks quietly and appears at a loss for what to do.

I tell him that his parents love him and want the best for him but, in a divorce, they're going through hell and can't help but focus on each other, especially if there's lingering ill will. I tell him straight out that this probably won't change very soon. I tell him that while it may not seem evident, his parents do need him, and he has to find a way to stay close, which will make him feel better. He tells me he's been seeing a counselor, which his mother had told me. I endorse that idea, discussing the benefits, without telling him I've seen one, too.

We talk for a while. I grow animated when I tell him how he can use his troubles for strength on the racecourse. So far, the issues have weakened him. I explain how people overcome their problems not by using them as a crutch but as empowerment to achieve something, if only to prove it can be done. "Take charge," I say. "Make it work for you, not against you. It doesn't mean the problem's gone. But you're better able to deal with it."

Ryan tries to be stoic but his expression turns forlorn and I feel a profound sadness. This boy has so much to offer but is cheated by the disease of divorce, which is so common we don't realize its grave effects. Ryan is smart and strong beyond his years. Mental-health day? That's so cool. He got it right. I know Ryan can be a great runner, that he can rally our team and inspire the coach as well.

As the team returns from its run, we wrap it up and Ryan tells me he's going to a hockey game tonight with his father. I insist he speak up and discuss what's hurting him. Tell your mom too, I suggest; don't keep your feelings hidden. I say I'll speak to Mom and Dad myself.

Ryan gets on his bike and leaves. I worry whether my advice will help. But I feel it's important for Ryan to know I'm in his corner. On the drive home, still seeing Ryan's forlorn face, I can't help but bawl like a baby.

7

Oceangate

Karen Lavender turns up to power-walk the Belmar boards, then wait to take Ryan home from practice. The team has not arrived yet, so Mom and I can talk. Mom says Ryan is doing better, letting his feelings be known. "He's adjusting," she says. Karen has a sunny outlook through it all and I give her credit for that. We agree that Ryan's running will serve as a reflection of his progress at home and that I'll keep a close watch on him for telltale signs. Karen delivers me a sign I'm not happy with. She asks if Ryan told me that he ran a five-mile road race last Sunday. No, he hasn't, and no, he wouldn't say so. Ryan knows I forbid that during the season. No extra racing, especially on concrete; you just risk injury and burnout.

"Ryan didn't really race," Karen says. "He just ran hard."

I think Ryan competed for a confidence boost after his modest effort against Mater Dei. He wanted to prove to himself that he still had the makings of a good runner. I decide not to take it up with him. Unless Ryan comes down with an injury. Then I'll scream.

When the boys arrive, I emphasize that we cannot take Mater Dei for granted when it comes to the state meet. It's early October and we have six weeks to our big day. Complacency could kill us. To stir the boys, I announce that we have a potential new state rival in Montclair Kimberley, whose top runner, Oskar Nordenbring, is a freshman known as "the Swede."

Nordenbring was born in Sweden. With Montclair coached by former New York City Marathon winner Tom Fleming, Nordenbring and his teammates have been collecting victories and the squad is gaining on us in the *Star-Ledger* state parochial school rankings.

"The Swede," I say. "He may be a freshman but he can run."

Brock's already heard of him through the internet. The boys bring up other teams, other athletes. After three years, the boys are finally showing interest in our opposition. Previously, my statewide pronouncements would fall on deaf ears. Now the boys are the ones keeping tabs on teams from outside our area like Wildwood Catholic of South Jersey, 1998 state winner when my boys were freshmen and St. Rose placed a distant third. Wildwood's not a contender this season.

"How good is the Swede?" asks Solebello.

I tell the boys what I know and say that now Brock and Ryan will have competition for the individual state championship. Thus far, I've been downplaying individual goals while stressing the team goals. Brock or Ryan could win the gold medal. But my message is always this: Run for the team and individual success will follow. The converse, however, is not true. Run for yourself and you'll lose sight of the team.

I don't have to worry about Brock. He's a team player who will not do anything rash, in practice or competition, to jeopardize team chances. Whether it's holding the right pace, sticking with another runner, or employing a particular strategy, Brock can be counted on to come through. Brock sees his success and the team's as one and the same.

Ryan has more talent but looks at running differently. It's not only because of family issues; it's his nature. Ryan, I believe, sees himself apart from the team—as its leader through superiority rather than comradeship. This is a valid vision. But it's a vision accompanied by risk, and that worries me.

Risk may be the whole point. "The Irish nature is characterized by talent without discipline." That would be a questionable summation if not told to me by the patron saint of Irish runners, Noel Carroll. I was in Dublin some years ago doing a profile of Eamonn Coghlan, the Irish track legend who became the first man forty or older to break the four-minute mile. I made a point of visiting Carroll, a former Olympian himself who could wax poetic about running and the Irish legacy.

At the time, Carroll was the public-relations director for the city of Dublin and I sat down with him at City Hall. "Eamonn is a classic example of that," Carroll said about the intemperate Irish approach. "When the bullets start flying, this nature emerges. We don't have the discipline to be fearful."

To draw Ryan in, I more firmly link him with Brock, even if that separates the pair from the rest of the team. We've got two stars, there's no need to hide that as though everyone's equal. I need to use Brock's and Ryan's strength to bolster each other, not merely as a catalyst for the others. Enough of this we-can-all-be-the-best. That's over. We have two best. Everyone else can try to catch up.

The other day, in a practice of repeat miles (our 0.9-mile course) on the boardwalk, I'd instructed Brock and Ryan to run at the front "with their skin touching" and shoot for times below five minutes. I told the other guys not to get sucked in but if anyone could stick close to our two stars—that's what I called them, "stars"—and show big improvement, fine.

Brock and Ryan ran as one. They reeled off times of 4:48, 5:22 (into the wind), and 4:57. They brushed shoulders and elbows. Neither surged ahead or gave in. It was a beautiful thing to see the two boys run hard together. They looked so content. I was in Heaven. And I was beyond Heaven when Gallagher stuck close, throwing his moodiness into the sea and ripping it on the boards. His times were 4:52, 5:28, and 5:14, the best he'd ever run. I whooped it up, slapping backs, saying, yeah, this is how great we can run. The boys drank, and enjoyed the afterglow. Gallagher looked more assured, like he was part of the team, not some ghostly figure looking in.

Back at the lake with the Point Beach dual meet the next day, the assessment of our state field continues when Brock says Bishop Eustace has been switched from the large-school Parochial A division, the one with CBA, to our B race. I shrug it off, saying keep running as well you have in practice and Bishop Eustace will have to worry about us.

I'm hot on Gallagher. He tells me he ran again before school. Four-point-eight miles, no more, no less. I wish I could have seen it. I'm hot on Dunn. He's running with authority on consecutive days. Right now, I'm feeling hot on the whole team. Brock and Ryan are my Simon and Garfunkel. Solebello's on a roll after his Mater Dei PR. Ruhl is so fired up he ran a 5:38, then two low sixes in the recent repeat miles, his best practice by far. Leschak's times quicken as his spiked hair shoots skyward. He looks like a *Saturday Night Live* character but runs Holmdel practices like an animal. A divine order has blessed the squad and I think coaching boys, even with their bad-ass humor, is a lot more fun than coaching girls, who sit in a perfect circle while stretching and always do what you say.

I feel the team has surrendered itself to me. It started in Charlotte, but there the boys were lulled into submission by being away. Now we're on home turf, consumed in the everyday. By showing more responsibility and trying harder, the boys open the door wider, entering the world I want for them, the otherworld that can make the Bowl feel like a piece of cake.

The Swede? No problem.

I feel powerful. I have the team in my grasp. These guys are no longer fighting right-mindedness. They know the right thing—not for me, for them—and are doing it. They are running, not just because the coach says so, but because they want to from some deep place within.

"Let's get off the grass," says Ryan after the warm-up around the lake.

He's the boss. Whoever speaks up is the boss. That's how much I want to trust them. We stretch on the uncomfortably hard board-walk instead of the lake grounds because Canada geese rule the lake. Their droppings carpet the grass and there's not a clean spot to be found. There are so many geese that they block the running path around the lake. They've become so bold that they barely move when the boys' strides threaten to stomp them.

I read in the papers that the Canada goose population has exploded across the country. New Jersey, which leads the league in dubious distinctions (our political cronyism is off the charts), has a hundred thousand geese, the most of any state. Seems like half of them have congregated in Belmar. Though the geese foul parks, damage crops, contaminate water supplies, and threaten airport safety, they are protected by federal laws. Signs at the lake read the riot act to those who might tamper with these privileged creatures.

No one knows what to do about them. The lake is an ideal meeting place for the team. It has benches where I set up my paperwork and the boys line up their water bottles. The boys sit and we can talk in private. The boardwalk is too open and windy, but that's where we have to go to avoid goose crap.

For stretching space, the boys tuck behind a clubhouse, the Fifth Avenue Pavilion, a social hall for senior citizens. The back has a porch facing the beach and people sit on rocking chairs watching the surf. The older folks tell me how cute and respectful the boys are; one time, an octogenarian is heard telling her friend that I'm cute and it takes me weeks to live that one down.

I wear my St. Rose sweatshirt and suspect locals assume I'm Catholic, which gives me a perverse satisfaction. I get waves and nods from proprietors along the beach and feel part of the Belmar community, alluring in its fall quiet, erotic in the way it offers forbidden hopes once you cross the Shark River Bridge and enter its vacation habitat.

Shark River is an old drawbridge. No matter how precisely I time my trip to the school, almost every afternoon when I get to the bridge it's in the process of opening to let the taller fishing boats through. The wait is about seven minutes and causes quite a backup. There's further congestion from construction of a new bridge that will provide better access to the Belmar marina.

Belmar's population of six thousand swells to fifty thousand in the summer, when police have to patrol the beach strip monitoring young visitors who drink themselves silly. I find the fall quiet like a sedative. On the business strip, patrons of the taverns and tackle shops, bakeries and Chinese takeouts, move about at a confident pace, aware that this town is their own and that with the pleasures of the sea nearby things will take care of themselves.

The boys stretch and some go onto the sand for sit-ups. Solebello tells me he ran over the weekend during his hunting trip to Pennsylvania. Excellent. I've never hunted, and I ask him about it. Mike explains that he and his dad hunted deer with a bow and arrow. His story fascinates me and I invite Mike to give me the details. He enjoys telling me how they bag their prize and how his dad skins and quarters the deer right in the woods, leaving the carcass for the rest of the animal kingdom. Then they have the deer meat for dinner.

Mike speaks in a thoughtful, earnest way as though teaching a class. He avoids the truncated teenage idiom. Step by step, Mike describes the hunt while showing humanity, a concern for nature and the world around him. He likes order and discipline, and no carelessness escapes him. In North Carolina, Mike had the gall— God bless him—to slap me on the wrist for a casual remark I'd made about a girl they'd met who was grazed by a motorist and sent to the hospital. The girl, who ran for a team in New Hampshire, was not so much hurt as shaken up. I said something glib about the incident and when we were alone Mike suggested that maybe I was being unfair to the girl. I told him he was right and apologized.

The day in Belmar is great: It's sunny and warm like summer and the boys pull off their shirts for running. The team is relaxed with little more than jogging at hand. They can all run together, their hearts almost at rest, and talk shop. Tomorrow's meet with Point Beach on our home course should be an easy win. I send the boys off for some stride-outs around the lake, then 2.2 miles up and down the boards for 3 miles in all. I want them fully rested for the meet. It's important for us to run hard on our home course because in a few weeks we'll face our toughest dual-meet opponent,

Rumson-Fair Haven, at home with the conference title on the line.

I start my watch and expect the boys back in around twenty-three or twenty-four minutes. I kill time walking the boards and gazing at the ocean. Retirees with golden tans sit on the beach soaking up the good weather. No one's in the water except surfers down in Spring Lake. The rustling surf kicks up against the shore with a music that almost puts me to sleep. Cops come by on bike patrol. They're young and clean-cut, like actors in a beach movie. We make small talk. I check my watch. The guys should be back soon.

I run two blocks to a deli for a soda, wait some more, and look south down the boards in case the boys appear early. They don't. Time passes. I have twenty-five minutes on the watch. Karen Lavender comes by finishing her walk. She has the crimson complexion of exercise completed. I ask her if she's seen the guys or maybe noticed Ryan. She hasn't.

We wait together joking about the team and where they could be. She says boys will be boys so who knows. I say someone might have needed a bathroom and since most bathrooms along the shore are locked up or even carted away after Labor Day, that's probably it, they had to search for a bathroom, maybe duck into the Dunkin' Donuts. Or, God forbid, someone got injured, had to stop, and the whole team is walking it in.

I pray someone had to take a shit.

My watch is past thirty minutes and I'm walking the boards, looking, looking, but no team. I squint for Lavender's blond locks, the best sighting from a distance. Karen waits, too, and is amused as I stand there talking to myself, checking my watch every few seconds, thinking, *Why the hell is it when you assign the easiest workout ever, 1.1 miles to the Spring Lake border and back, 2.2 miles round trip, the team is nowhere to be found?* Their hearts may be at rest but mine is jumping.

156

Usually, I drive to the turnaround point to see how the team is doing, and for this very reason—in case something is amiss. I figured, for a couple of miles, why bother, leave them alone. Now I think they got into a fight. Yes, a fight. Because even if they were walking they'd be here by now. Because my fucking watch says thirty-eight minutes and forty-five seconds!

I always tell them to be careful on the boards. Don't get in anyone's way. You guys don't own the boards. Give people the right-of-way. Watch for parents pushing baby carriages. Don't challenge other kids who stand their ground blocking your path. Go around them. Don't mess with other teams who come over from rough neighborhoods. Avoid confrontation. Don't wind up in a fight.

So they got into a fight, that's it, why else would my watch be over forty minutes and no boys? These strong-legged but basically scrawny guys in a fight? And with me in charge. I'm responsible. You let teenage boys out of your sight for a minute and see what happens.

And then, at forty-five minutes and counting, I spot Lavender coming toward me. It's the hair. The group, yes, I see the outline of the group. I make them out one by one and I wait anxiously to find out why it took them an extra twenty minutes to jog from the Fifth Avenue Pavilion in Belmar to the Arches in Spring Lake and back.

As they close in on me, I do a quick count and all seven boys are present. Lavender is barefoot and his hair is wet and disheveled. Dunn too, and Leschak: barefoot, carrying their shoes, hair wet and messed.

"So . . . what happened?"

Speaking for the group, Lavender explains that they were running along about half a mile down the boards toward home when they spotted a man caught in a riptide. Lavender (a lifeguard in the summer) and a couple of the other guys tore off their shoes to rush into the surf to rescue the man. And the other boys went with them for support, so the whole team was involved in saving this guy, whom Lavender describes as "Chinese."

Lavender's description is muddled and I can't tell exactly who went into the water and who stood on the sand watching. I press for details but get few. I ask if the police were present. Not really. Despite the vagueness and the oddly crooked expressions I notice—and the fact that the boys don't quite look me in the eye—I'm relieved no one was hurt and proud of these good Samaritans who apparently saved a man's life.

The boys quickly drop the subject and do their final stretches. I congratulate them on their bravery and wonder aloud why they're so nonchalant about their heroic act, which is probably the most important thing they've done as St. Rose students and the kind of story that could wind up being the talk of the Shore.

"It's really no big deal," insists Lavender.

But I think it is and that night when I happen to speak to Jim Lambert, who covers high school cross-country for the *Star-Ledger*, I tell him what happened. I also plan to notify school authorities. These boys deserve credit, and it wouldn't hurt Lavender, who seems to have led the rescue, to get some good press. Lambert's impressed and says he'll mention the episode in a small item in the paper and asks if it's okay to call Lavender for an interview. Of course. After speaking with Lavender, Lambert calls me back and says his editor wants a feature story on the rescue and the paper would like to send a photographer to the school tomorrow to get a shot of the team at the beach. That'll be tricky with our meet scheduled, but we work out the details and I thank Jim for his consideration.

I call Lavender with the good news and ask him to take charge in rounding up the boys after class for the photo shoot. He's subdued, then says again, "It's really not that big a deal." I tell him it sure is, don't be so modest, and the publicity will be great for the school.

The next morning while working in my home office I get a call from Dick Alger, the St. Rose athletic director. He says, "Marc, we have a problem."

Dick proceeds to inform me that he heard what happened yesterday at the beach and the story the boys told was a fabrication. If anyone was saved it was one or more of my boys. Dick says the kids impulsively ran off the boardwalk and into the water; someone got caught in a riptide and had to be pulled out of trouble by a team member. He's not sure who did what. Dick's voice is low. He's not accusatory but somber. He does not express anger toward the boys, or me. For him, it's more like another day at school when kids transgress, and after Dick hangs up with me he'll put out the next fire.

Me? I'm out of control. I unleash my fury on the phone with Dick. I say I'd pull the boys out of today's Point Beach meet except I know I can't do that, it's a conference obligation. I need an immediate punishment so Dick will know I won't stand for this and I can satisfy my abundant need for revenge. I decide to withdraw the team from Saturday's Shore Coaches Invitational meet at Holmdel Park. It's a big event the boys are looking forward to. Dick says fine, it's up to me, and we'll talk more later.

Goddamnfuckingkids.

I'm a mess. My entire physical being changes. I walk from room to room as anger and frustration and disillusionment build. I want to explode. I walk out of the house and down the block hoping no neighbor sees me in this state. I come back and try to settle down. I can't. I'm bewildered. I'm hurt. Personally hurt. I take this act of defiance as a personal affront. This is a huge blow and I feel a profound letdown. In short: betrayed.

I place my hopes with these boys. I give them my best. I trust them. I treat them like they're my own flesh and blood. I teach them everything I know. I embrace them when they're down. I buy them Dunkin' Donuts. For what?

I want to quit. That'll show them. I'll quit. I don't need this. The hell with them. Let them coach themselves. I devote myself to these kids and this is the thanks I get? How stupid are they? They run into the ocean and someone almost drowns! I picture a scene where medics drag a boy's body out of the water and parents are gathered around and the whole community is in mourning—all because the coach took his eye off the team for an instant.

Is it me? What *didn't* I do? Where did I go wrong? How did I let them down? What message could I have given them that would allow for such criminal behavior?

Or was this inevitable? God, was I wrong about kids? I thought I could set them straight. I thought anyone could learn the right way. If I'm wrong about these kids, then I'm wrong about life. So much of the faith I have in humanity is wrapped up these kids who show me—at least they did up to now—that I can make a difference and in a small way, as written in the Hebrew text, "bring a light to the nations."

I call Jim Lambert at home to call off the *Star-Ledger* photo session. I reach him in the nick of time and apologize for the episode. Jim's okay with it. I call Karen Lavender to see if she knows anything more but can't reach her.

I drop my work, collect my gear, and head to the YMCA pool. A swim is the only thing that could possibly relax me. I spend an hour in the pool mapping out my tongue-lashing sermon to the boys. The rhythmic strokes calm me and the comforting water brings some clarity. The speech has to be perfect. My words have to be heartfelt and precise. There can be no equivocating on the gravity of what took place, what they boys did, and how I feel about it. They must learn a lesson. And they must be punished.

The rest of the season? Right now I only care about righting a wrong. I can't believe sixteen-year-old boys who live at the beach, who know the ocean like a wolf knows the prairie, would risk life and limb in the turbulent surf. And then lie about it. The great cover-up. Oceangate.

I swim and swim and swim. I try to let the water and my thoughts blend in a purifying revelation. I know I bruise easily and tend to react hard. I don't take kindly to rejection. That people will not always reciprocate kindness is for me one of life's tougher lessons. These are still kids, for whom physical prowess and emotional maturity are not equal partners. Every day they must confront the real unreal world that broadcasts macho insolence as the ultra-cool male mindset.

I picture the boys one by one and see their smiles. I remind myself how wonderful they are and that we are a family. We have amassed blistering work at running and beyond together. We have not run to excess—if anything, we could be doing more—but we have not had much comic relief, either. Maybe that was it. With intensified training toward the state meet imminent, maybe the boys decided to have their own version of a toga party, and get it out of their system, like soldiers going into battle, as a last hurrah. Where else but at the water where they live?

I sort out my feelings. I'm less hurt now. I'm still wounded but leaning toward conciliation, not condemnation; on teaching a lesson, not kicking some butt. The atonement messages of Yom

Kippur, a few days before, are still with me. Atonement is not a free pass. You have to earn it. I rehearse my lecture and on the way to St. Rose worry most about holding my emotional grip. It's all right for the boys to see me emotional; the occasion calls for it. But I don't want to be teary. I want to be tough and unwavering but give the boys enough wiggle room to make amends. We have to straighten this out and move on. Maybe even some good can come of it.

When the boys see me at St. Rose, they lower their heads and look away. I have them assemble on the steps of a free standing school building out of view of passing students. They sit hunched up and fearful, knowing they did wrong, I stand before them and say, "Okay, who's going to tell me what happened?"

Ryan Lavender pipes up and evenly, as though reciting a composition, tells the tale. I'm glad Lavender's the one to speak up. He says that toward the end of the run they all talked about going into the water. And after they did they were afraid of my reaction and decided to make up a story. No one else says a word or lifts his head.

In a cracking voice, I tell them that the lie was worse than the deed. It always is. I bring up the examples of Nixon and Bill Clinton and say it was their attempted cover-ups that got them into the worst trouble. I tell them as bad as the boys' act was, it's the lie that is the worse sin, compounding the guilt. The lie makes it personal and is more a reflection of character. The act shows a lapse in judgment, the lie indicates intent. It shows an unwillingness to face the music. A lack of courage. I say, "You're runners, you should have courage."

And I tell them how disappointed I am in them—how they let me down as well as their parents and the school. How they let themselves down. I tell them they hurt people and that someone could have died in the ocean. I tell them how shocked I am that with their experience at the beach they would put themselves at such risk. I tell them that the whole sorry episode devalues them.

They sit and take it. Finally, I bring up Yom Kippur and explain how just the other day I was in prayer atoning for my sins. I remind them that forgiveness is a central concept in Catholic teaching as well. I say, "We are human, we make mistakes, we seek redemption. But to be redeemed, you must not only confess but show contrition. Today you've confessed. It's a start."

I explain that after today's meet, I am not going to hold a team practice for a week. "You can run on your own. It's up to you." I tell them to spend the week contemplating their act and how to respond further. Write letters of apology to Dick Alger and to Jim Lambert at the *Star-Ledger*. And we will withdraw from the Shore Coaches Invitational on Saturday at Holmdel. With its statewide entry, the meet is important for us but we don't deserve to compete.

The boys seem relieved that it's all come out and their punishment is not worse. I'm relieved, too, that I made my points and struck the right tone. The last thing we need right now is a race, but Point Beach is waiting so we hustle over to our home course in Wall Township.

Our cross-country course at the St. Rose Athletic Field connects from a series of open fields to a wooded tract abutting Allaire Airport. The course is challenging because the scrub-pine trails are largely ungroomed, in the natural state that cross-country was founded on. You run through the wilds. There are heavy grass and sand and deep crevices that will swallow you whole if you don't watch your step. When it rains, the sand shifts and suddenly you have to run right instead of left. The crevices widen to the size of craters. Portions of the running path become impassable, or least too risky for ankles to withstand without popping.

Ankles that avoid popping are still vulnerable to the wildlife. One day after a practice run at the site, the boys come up to me with some news. "Coach," they say in unison. "Snakes."

Every summer I have to inspect the site and report back to Dick Alger on what I see. Dick then hires a local guy who comes with a bulldozer to refashion the course and make it runable. The course is never exactly the same as in the previous year. Even the distance changes. One year it's 3 miles, the next year 2.8. For that reason, we can't keep legitimate course records.

From November when our season ends to the following September, the place can be radically different. We confront not only the elements but also the eccentric man who owns Allaire Airport and the grounds we run on as well as local outdoorsmen, who pose the biggest threat of all.

Last year when I did my preseason inspection, I found a huge rectangular boulder sitting on the course blocking the running path. The airport owner, Ed Brown, an irascible man in his eighties, apparently put it there to block township vehicles from entering. He had nothing against St. Rose. He's in constant battle with local officials over the management of the airport and its grounds. The ill will goes back decades. The town would like to purchase the airport but Brown won't sell.

This season we are presented with the biggest surprise yet. When I check the course I find a new hangar smack on our route. Just like that—this building the size of a football field and a concrete access area replacing portions of the dirt path. Brown, a former navy pilot who practically built the airport himself in the forties, is in a public brawl over the hangar, too. Apparently, Brown did not bother to get building permits from the town.

This being our first home meet of the season, the boys have

questions when I send them off on their warm-up loop in the woods. Like, what's our racecourse exactly? Will we run left or right around the hangar? And with that new concrete section should we still wear spikes? Spikes slow you down on a hard surface but are essential on the dirt trails.

I get annoyed when we face these issues because most teams like us without school grounds for a home course, like Mater Dei and Keansburg, use Holmdel Park for their site, paying the county a fee. But these fields are Dick's pride and joy. He and his crew have nurtured the ball fields like daylilies. The grounds have gone from a rutted mess to manicured greens. The fields have spiffy painted borders and spectator bleachers and there's a new equipment shed. I once lost my head and inadvertently drove my car over the soccer field, putting tire marks on Dick's turf. He wanted to crucify me.

But I've got bigger problems now. The boys come back from their warm-up with news. "Hunters," they report in unison. "We saw hunters shooting at birds."

Hunters with rifles on the cross-country course. If my boys don't drown in the sea, they'll be shot in a race. Dick is not around to hear this. I grab the school trainer, Melinda, and haul ass in her golf cart to the woods to check it out. Sure enough, we find two guys in full hunting regalia. They're wary because they're breaking the law. I politely explain that we have a meet and that a bunch of teenagers, boys and girls, will be coming through shortly. They don't want any trouble so they agree to pack up and leave. At least that's what they say.

I don't share this with the many parents who have gathered to confer over the beach incident. I hear them buzzing and tell them we'll talk after the race. The boys say nothing and I say little. We need time to let the chill dissipate and I just want to get this race out of the way cleanly with no mishap. We know we're going to win. The meet will function like an intrasquad race.

The teams line up together, boys and girls. Point Beach, located farther south down the shore in Point Pleasant, has only one decent runner on their boys' team. I enlist parents to help with scoring. Karen Lavender will give the finishing runners numbered Popsicle sticks indicating their place. After catching their breath, the athletes will return the sticks to Sue Solebello, who will record the names and places on the clipboard I gave her. I'll be at the finish calling out times for Sue to write next to the boys' names.

The official fires the starting gun and my boys string out on the opening path around the soccer fields leading to the woods. A locked fence protects the woods from intruders, but there are ways to get around the fence, as hunters have discovered. I have to unlock, and then lock up, the fence at every meet. This is no rahrah day. I'm not inclined to cheer the boys or decipher lessons for the climactic Rumson-Fair Haven encounter later in the month. I run into the woods to make sure the hunters have gone.

Lavender is first, with a good lead over Silvestri. Then it's Gallagher, Dunn, Solebello, Ruhl, and Leschak for St. Rose. Point Beach has its top boy in third. The rest of the Point Beach squad is far back. The boys do two loops of the same counterclockwise path. Their spikes click on the new concrete section. Cones mark the key turns. At one point the path veers close to the airport runway and we see planes taking off and landing. Probably going to Atlantic City.

I check for hunters, and snakes. All clear.

The positions don't change. Lavender's firmly ahead as though he has something to prove. Since he had the biggest role in the ocean scam, perpetuating the lie as the newspaper story evolved, I think he wants to show me something with his run and perhaps cleanse himself as well. Lavender brings it home first and I'm happy to see him chalk up a victory. His time is 16:17 for 2.8 miles. Silvestri finishes about seventy-five yards back in 16:30. Gallagher runs well but can't catch the Point Beach boy and takes fourth. We take eight of the top nine spots. Even Leschak, our last man in, outruns all but one of the opposition.

The score is St. Rose 18, Point Beach 45. We're 2-0 in our league. I make sure the boys shake hands with the Point Beach guys. It's a ritual even the losers like.

Dunn and Gallagher come up to me to apologize.

"I accept your apology, thank you."

The boys do their cool-down and I gather the parents, who form a circle around me. Some parents are up to date, others know little. I outline what happened, saying how stunned I was, how hurt I felt, how everything was going so famously before this. I don't mention any boy by name but indict the team as one and review the punishment. The parents, whom I respect, every last one of them, apologize as though they are at fault. I don't want that. I tell them I don't hold them responsible and we'll just have to move on. Michael Dunn's mother says she knew the story and upbraided her son last night.

With teary eyes, I tell the parents, who touch me as ever with their support, that the whole matter is too difficult to discuss any further right now and I'll see them in a week.

That night, Ryan calls me to apologize and thank me for the help I've been giving him. Brock also calls. He wants me to know it was not his idea to run into the ocean and that he didn't want to go along with it but got drawn in with the group. I tell him not to worry, I suspected that all along, but I could not exclude him from the blame or punishment. He understands. He wouldn't want that. Which I also know.

With a week off, I have time to come to terms with the crisis. I try to let my rational self take hold. Maybe I am now less rabid about molding these boys into perfect runners and perfect beings. I become more accepting of our destiny, inevitably flawed, and realize I cannot make up for any disorder in my life, or in the world around me, by creating idealized harmony within the St. Rose cross-country team.

The boys are too smart to be perfect. Have they shown me with their foolish act that the risks they took, not only with the sea but with adult comeuppance as well, demonstrate a wildness compatible with cross-country itself? Was there some recognition in their subconscious that good soldiers will not necessarily win the day? That a restless challenge to authority will somehow play itself out to our gain on the cross-country course? I wonder if the boys have accrued some obscure genius that could prove to override the coaching handbook. Ryan Lavender a genius? I wouldn't doubt it.

Every day, these boys teach me something new. I just hope they run on their own this week. And I hope I get no more calls from Dick Alger saying, "Marc, we have a problem."

A day later, the following e-mail on behalf of the team arrives from the Solebello household:

Dear Coach Bloom,

All of us on the team want to apologize for our actions. We not only endangered our lives but we disappointed you, humiliated ourselves in front of the *Star-Ledger*, and embarrassed our school.

We value the time, effort, and heart that you have given

to our cross-country team. You have made us what we are today. We may be small in numbers, but with you behind us inspiring us to do our best we're doing great.

We cannot take back what has already happened but we can promise that it will not happen again. We will try to regain your trust by our future actions and hope that we can make you proud.

Respectfully, the entire cross-country team

I am a man. But my boys have reduced me to mush as I read their words over and over, savoring their sentiment. I feel so proud of them already. It is they who inspire me. I return the message with these words:

Dear Mike D, Justin, Ryan, John, Chris, Brock, Mike S,

Thank you for your well-thought-out letter. You've done well sorting out your feelings and expressing them with sincerity and understanding. You've taken some big steps here. Apology is not an easy process. It's hard enough for adults; for young people it shows courage and humanity, qualities we always talk about on our team. Sometimes, a situation like this can make people stronger. Let's put the episode behind us and move to do our best, on and off the field. Keep running, and I'll see you next Tuesday.

Sincerely, Coach Bloom

I'm convinced that fate delivered Oceangate. I think we are stronger for it, closer, more in sync, more ready to meet the challenges ahead. I feel renewed faith that good things will happen, that faith makes them happen. As it is written in Lamentations: "They are new every morning: great is your faithfulness."

With my enlightenment, I go to the Shore Coaches meet at Holmdel to check on our rivals. I'm rooting for them because competition is what we desire. I'm not disappointed. Bishop Eustace runs well. And Montclair Kimberley runs well, led by the Swede.

8

The Pizza Race

To regain our rhythm, hard work with a light touch, I challenge Justin Gallagher, who's lagging lately no matter how much I try to light his fire. I can tell he did little running during the week of penitence. Mike Solebello is outrunning him in practice. Solebello has never beaten Gallagher in a race. That could change soon. I tell Gallagher Solebello's going to kick dust in his face in our meet against Keansburg tomorrow at Holmdel. He shrugs like *Nice try, Coach*. Solebello smiles but says nothing. The other guys crowd around enjoying my threat.

We're practicing at the lake and boardwalk. It's glove weather. A few guys still dress like summer. Others welcome fall, the time for cross-country. Chris Ruhl is not here. He's at a Yankee game. Since Chris is a ballplayer at heart, I let it go. Anyone else, I'd bitch like mad. John Leschak is not here. The guys say he's coming late. He doesn't show. I find out he was held in detention. I'm not surprised. At St. Rose, Leschak is like a bucking bronc. He cannot be confined. Maybe he wore the wrong tie or no tie, or wised off. Whatever his offense, I'm sure it was without calculation. It was just Leschak, the mad hatter who will one day save the world.

Ryan Lavender's lagging worse than Gallagher. He's got a history of sinus problems, which have grown worse, and he uses inhalers daily. I'm convinced stress can bring on sinus problems but keep that view to myself. Lavender goes for a sinus X-ray. Sinus, schminus. The kid's up and down depending on personal issues. The other day when he did 5 x 1100 meters around the lake, a staple workout, Lavender crapped out like my first car. He did 3:33, then the rest over 4:00, and chalked it up to swollen sinuses. Solebello did the team's best running behind Brock, and that showed me he was ready to take on Gallagher. Gallagher ran 3:42, 3:52, 3:52, then 4-and-change when he stopped to tie his shoe, and 3:51. Solebello ran 3:37, 3:43, 3:43, 3:46, 3:44. Laces tied tight. Beautiful.

"If Solebello beats you in the Keansburg meet," I tell Gallagher, "you owe me a pizza, which I will share with Mike. If you beat him, I owe you a pie."

Gallagher says, okay Coach, and smiles. I can tell I've got him thinking. And I can also tell—unfortunately—that this pizza will be mine.

Solebello also outpracticed Michael Dunn, who comes up to me today and says, "What am I gonna do to get better, Coach?" Sincerity, I like that. I run down the list, emphasizing confidence because Mike still thinks of himself as a little boy in the shadow of his high-achieving sisters. I tell him he's stronger than he thinks, that he's a natural runner settling for less than his best. I wish I could be more specific, more clinical, but so much of running success is based on clarifying the vagueness of your powers. You think and think and think and finally you "see" what has existed all along: a kind of personal majesty. Someday I will crown him King Michael.

Today's workout revisits the scene of the crime. It's the same easy session we did on the day of infamy: some sprints around the lake and 2.2 miles up and back on the boards to Spring Lake. A way to show my trust. As the boys said, Oceangate will never happen again. And even though Keansburg is a weak opponent, I want the boys rested for the Holmdel hills. They have to get used to putting out with fresh legs with the state meet a month away.

I wait for our momentum to return. Collective consistency. Everybody pushing every day for a week. No Yankee games. No sinuses. No detention. I realize I have to be more accepting of the inconsistency of teenage boys. If we're up one day, I'm on a high; if we're down the next, I crumble and feel we're lost. But I can't forget we have been stockpiling right-thinking like weapons—virtues that can lead to superiority. I cherish little things, like when Lavender mocks his cousin for being allowed to drive a fancy car to school. The boy gets it.

What none of them seem to get, despite their religious education, is that all people deserve equal respect. When they see the occasional black kids on the boardwalk, remarks are made. When they see Hasidic Jewish boys with side curls ride their bikes up from the orthodox enclave in Bradley Beach, remarks are made. Some remarks are innocent enough—the "my boss is a Jewish carpenter" variety. I've heard a lot worse from kids. But I can't help feeling that by embracing everyone you form a covenant with God. You exalt yourself, feel more comfortable in your own skin. You take that to Holmdel Park and the Bowl becomes flatter. As someone once said, all you need is love.

I tell the boys that. To make my points, I lavish my "Julio" story on them, in segments at a time. How as a young track writer not much older than they I immersed myself in the black world of high school track, traveling throughout the New York area and around the country with athletes like Julio Meade, who starred at Andrew Jackson High School in Cambria Heights, Queens. How I hung around the Jackson track watching Meade, who grew up dirt-poor in the Dominican Republic and didn't speak a word of English when he came to New York but excelled through the sheer force of his will. How I went on the Boys High bus from Bed-Stuy in Brooklyn to a meet in Schenectady and none of the black athletes wanted to room with me so the coach stuck me with the only Hispanic kid, who twenty years later saw me at a road race and gave me a hug.

As an innocent on the track beat, I was confronted with a full menu of black culture, which I embraced not for its coolness but for its honesty and spirit. Julio Meade, in particular, was smarter, tougher—and more generous—than anyone I knew. In June 1966, Julio was Golden West national high school champion in the 440-yard dash. I traveled with Julio and others to the championships in Sacramento, California. It was my first flight. We took a side trip to Tahoe, where we photographed each other with our Instamatics and dipped our toes into the frigid lake.

There were no Julios in my neighborhood. But Cambria Heights and Bed-Stuy entered my soul, and I've tried to give all people the humanity they deserved, which has disengaged me from those who would not. Twenty years later I would be linked forever in the track universe with Julio and his peers after writing a long piece about a high school record set by Andrew Jackson and Boys High in a photo-finish race that I alone witnessed among the press in 1966. The record was set in the 2-mile relay and still stands today thirty-four years later. All eight runners on the two teams ran their best times. That happens about as often as a total eclipse of the sun.

What Julio represented is what I try to instill in my boys. Triumph over adversity. Perseverance. Grace under pressure. And learning, always learning. A way to take the world beyond the parochial currents on this side of the Shark River and give all people a chance. I feel the boys' running and growing commitment has opened their minds, and I want to pour all this in; if their courage thus far puts them halfway up the Bowl, humanity will take them to its crest.

The boys listen hard. They seem struck by my lessons but remain silent. My story is not intended to invite response. What I yearn for is a commitment that shows respect for themselves and one another, which will demonstrate an immortal Julio presence, the best you can be. The closer the boys come to that standard, the larger their pure world grows while their trite, impure world shrinks, hopefully, one day, to extinction.

It's a magnificent fall day at Holmdel for the Keansburg meet. Sunny, blue skies, the air crisp, a bite of chill. San Diego at 6 P.M. I can't get enough of it. I breathe deeply to inhale the earth. For St. Rose, it's the Pizza Race. Gallagher vs. Solebello. We will dispose of Keansburg and I want the boys, who are short on hillwork, to get another Holmdel experience under their belts. They must be able to run the course by rote.

I decide to say nothing during the race. I try that every so often. I will study the boys, not cheer them. I like to watch them close up in the quiet of a dual meet, when their breathing is audible as they whoosh by. It's a treat.

The best news is Brock. He takes command with the dependability of an old Checker Cab and runs away with it in his best time: 17:32. Brock is the best athlete I've coached. He makes the most of his assets. He performs the task each race calls for. He thinks. Close up, I can see his mind working and his calculation from each Holmdel section to the next. How he saves something for the Bowl and roars up and over with panache, pumping all the way to the finish.

Lavender's sinus X-ray is negative but he's still sniffling. He's second about a minute behind but that's all I expect. In his shadow comes the beautiful Solebello, his dark eyes alert and satisfied, shaving another eleven seconds off his best time, in 18:35, and, most importantly, kicking dust in the face of a straining Gallagher in fourth.

Somebody owes me a pizza pie.

I go easy on Gallagher. I don't want to embarrass him more than he already is. We sweep the first five places and score a shutout, 15-40, extending our record to 3-0. I'm all over Brock and Solebello, saying Brock is now a contender for the individual state title—I know he won't abuse that status—and Solebello, a sprinter, is now our number-three man and deserving of the best pizza to be found on the Jersey Shore.

Quick call to Dad as I leave the park. I should spend more time with him but can't. He's up on the gossip at the rehab center, like which therapist is quitting or has dumped her boyfriend. He appreciates every little thing anyone does for him. He does not complain about his condition but about whether a chair is placed in the right spot in his room. I understand that fussiness under duress. That was me in my year from hell.

The next day after practice I bail out Gallagher and buy the pizza for the team to share. It's half pepperoni, half broccoli. I set the pie down on a bench at the lake and tell Gallagher he gets the last slice. Everyone digs in, favoring pepperoni, and when it's Gallagher's turn he winces, saying, "Coach, I'm allergic to broccoli."

Never heard of that, I tell him. I also tell him broccoli is the healthiest food you can eat. He smiles. When Gallagher takes the slice, he picks off the broccoli and flings it into the garbage. Then he devours the slice in seconds.

Today Dunn's my man. I'd given the boys a routine five-miler on the boards, telling them to come back in about thirty-five minutes. Dunn bolted ahead by himself and ran 33:19. He looked so easy doing it. I'm stunned by how much a pure runner Dunn is one day, and how he tells me he can't wait to quit running the next. Okay, inconsistency, I get it.

We're doing more visualization, picturing success, which the boys like and ask for. I suggest they imagine breaking through barriers. But Gallagher seems increasingly aloof, and sluggish in runs, and one day his father, Larry, shows up at practice in his painter's truck while the boys are out running. Larry tells me he's caught his son smoking pot and last night, after being confronted, Justin stormed out of the house and didn't come back. "I don't want to lose my son," Larry says tearfully.

Larry tells me he doesn't know what to do. When the boys finish running, Justin gives his father a perfunctory nod. I tell him to talk to his father as I pull the other guys to the side. Father and son exchange words, Larry gets back in his truck, and Justin walks away. Larry wants Justin to go home with him so they can straighten things out but the boy refuses. Larry looks at me with needy eyes. I tell him, okay, I'll give it a shot.

I put my arm around Justin's shoulder and tell him his father stopped work early to come see him because he cares about him. Forget about the rest of practice, go home and work it out with him. Brimming with tears, Justin says no, they'll work it out later. Now, I say. Now is the time to confront it. I tell him I'm a parent and this is what I would be doing with my kids. Your dad is very concerned and he loves you. I sense Justin easing off. I give him a crunching hug and say, "Go . . ." He grabs his belongings and gets in his father's truck and they drive away.

The only thing I say to the team is, "Justin will be running in tomorrow's meet." I decide to let the matter rest unless Larry Gallagher brings it up again.

The next day we're at Van Cortlandt Park in the Bronx for our second meet of four in an eight-day period. I fear we're pushing the envelope. But the meet is the Manhattan College high school invitational, the largest event of its kind, with nine thousand entries from twelve states, and I want the team to experience Van Cortlandt, known as the cross-country mecca. Every high school runner in the New York area cuts his teeth at Vanny, situated at 242nd Street and Broadway in the northwest Bronx where the city's IRT subway line ends.

Runners have been tackling the hilly 2.5-mile course for a century. My boys are not rested so I don't expect much. A time of thirteen minutes is the elite level and if you break fourteen, you're good. I hope for fourteenish, that's all, and that no one trips, as Brock did as a freshman, and tumbles down a hill. The course is vastly different from Holmdel. You start on long flats requiring early speed, and large fields of up to three hundred runners funnel to the narrow "cowpath" leading to the woods. Holmdel-style patience will do you no good. The hills come after about three-quarters of a mile and they're clumped together. The layout calls for a different rhythm than we're used to, and with the dense pack you can count on an elbow in the ribs. The course finishes with a long, flat homestretch where it's easy to think you're almost done but have a ways to go.

When I ran, I hated it. My first meet I had to stop and walk on the steepest incline, known as Cemetery Hill. I was too proud a sprinter to take cross-country seriously and looked forward to the hero sandwiches we bought at the deli on Broadway for the two-hour subway ride home. One summer I tried to get in shape for cross-country by running after working with Dad on his soda route. I could barely move.

I fill the boys in on Van Cortlandt lore, telling them about the greats who've run there, like Alberto Salazar, who covered the 2.5-mile course in 12:22 in pouring rain. When they ask me what my times were, I say not nearly as fast as you guys can run and leave it at that. I don't tell them I ran in what was indelicately called the "scrub" division in the early sixties. Smart psychology on the part of league officials.

We're competing in one of the seven boys' varsity divisions. In our race, there are thirty-seven teams, about 250 runners. Leschak uses the occasion to show up at the park in a full-length clownlike costume topped by a tall, striped hat, probably three feet high. He parades around the grounds like, *Hey, what's going on?* I imagine Leschak on a prominent team like, say, York of Illinois, where the coach Joe Newton frowns on long hair. Today Leschak is definitely the strangest guy in the Bronx. And the Bronx has some pretty strange characters.

Wouldn't you know it, Leschak runs the best of anyone on the team. He's the last guy in but his time, 16:05, shows he ran closest to his potential (and much faster than the coach ever did here). Brock leads St. Rose in 14:24 with Gallagher looking a lot better just a stride back in his best race and Lavender, Dunn and Solebello following. We're eleventh in the team standings. Not that bad on tired legs. The kids look really worn out. Brock is dizzy and has to be comforted with cold compresses on his neck. He sits with his head between his legs. We depart knowing we have two meets coming up, the first on the nastiest trails we face, the home course at Henry Hudson High in Atlantic Highlands.

It took a dangerous man to devise the Hudson 5K course at Hartshorne Woods State Park. The park is used for mountain biking and peaks on a bluff overlooking the bay. You can't run real cross-country there because there are no carved-out dirt running paths, just steep concrete roads that go up and up, and down, and up and up, and all around. It's like running the Bowl several times. There's just no need for that in a high school race, and the concrete makes it that much worse.

But the park sits near Hudson High, and coach Vinnie Whitehead, who seems like a gentle soul, takes full advantage of it as his lion's den. Two years ago, when my boys were freshmen, Hudson had a good team. When Vinnie's boys showed us the course, it was sticker shock. Hudson had us run the entire course as a warm-up. Then Hudson went through its elaborate stretching routine while we got chilled waiting. It was almost dark when the race started. We got creamed. Half the squad got injured. We arrived back at St. Rose with our wounded around nine o'clock. I got home wiped out at ten and my wife said, "You want to coach for *this?*"

Now we're back at The Monster, as I call it. We're much better than Hudson, which is having an off-year. I instruct the boys to use the race as good practice but hold back so we minimize risk of straining muscles on the hills. I tell the five top guys to run together, keying off one another and switching the lead like bike racers in the Tour de France. Running has a cousin in cycling, and the team strategies are similar. If you run in formation, you save as much as 7 percent of your energy from drafting, and you can be pulled along by superior teammates. As a team, you can control a race by setting your preferred pace, showing the opposition your rear and blocking the path, which is part of the game. CBA uses this strategy to dominate. When the Colts' midnight-blue jerseys cover the paths at the front of a field, few teams dare challenge them.

Even though shore traffic can make the trip to Hudson close to an hour, many parents turn out, including Larry Gallagher. He's taking it day by day with Justin. Karen Lavender, as buoyant as ever, brings a post-race treat for the team: Ring Dings. Her new friend, I find out, is now her fiancé. I learn from Bill Jasko, former St. Rose girls' coach and my closest buddy at the school, that Ryan is not taking this well. Jasko, whose views on kids, running, and education mirror mine, is my link to anything important going on in the building. He sees my boys all day long, teaches some of them in his math classes, and adds to my insight on how they're doing. Bill tells me that Gallagher is hanging out with the wrong crowd.

But we have a race to run, victories to collect, and a state championship weeks away. A part of me wants to tell Lavender to just run the meets and put all these diversions aside. I'm not convinced that this approach wouldn't work. But I don't. I nurture. Ryan's girlfriend, who runs for another team and is a top scorer, has come and obviously he wants to impress her. The boys do what I say. They forge to the front as a group, taking the hills together at practice speed as Hudson falls back. Ryan sets the pace. He looks great and seems to enjoy being in charge. Brock, Mike Dunn, and Justin follow in tow. Mike Solebello struggles on the ascents and is gapped. Chris Ruhl, after an early fall, trails the field. Leschak's not here: another detention.

I hustle with Vinnie Whitehead to follow the course. You can get lost in this place and never be found. I'm gleeful that we're crushing

Hudson on their turf but polite and encouraging to all. Suddenly, Ryan slips behind and Karen and I look at each another, stunned. It's not even a real race. Ryan makes no attempt to rejoin the front. Brock inches ahead for the victory with Justin and Mike Dunn two strides back, seventeen seconds to Ryan, and another twenty-five to Solebello. We sweep the first five positions for another shutout, 15-40, and run our record to 4-0.

Almost perfect. I say good job to everyone, we accomplished our goal and escaped with our lives on this minefield of a course. I don't say anything to Ryan in front of his girlfriend. When the team disperses I talk with Ryan and his mom in private. With her son standing there, Karen asks how he can do better. I say Ryan's in great shape, the problem is all mental.

I look at Ryan and say, "You're giving up on yourself."

To which Karen says, "What can he do about it?"

This is what I tell them: "You were our number one runner for two years when we competed in freshmen and soph races, and that came easily. There was no pressure. Whenever we won, whenever you won, we were considered precocious, a team for the future. We were 'only' freshmen or 'only' sophs. This season, you're juniors in the big time, and you're expected to lead our team to victory. I think in your mind you don't want to be depended on as the number one guy. If you perform below your potential and Brock beats you, then the idea is, of course Brock won, I'm not going all out, that's not the real me, I could win if I wanted to. You're choosing that path rather than performing your best, winning, and being counted on to win. Because if you're counted on to win, and don't, that's a worse fate, and you'll feel more hurt, more of a sense of loss. In other words, you imagine more risk in working your ass off than not working your ass off. You're not the first athlete to confront this."

That's my Psych 101 lesson for the day. Karen and Ryan listen. The question is still how to fix the problem. But I feel I've gone far enough. I end with: "Think about it."

Two days later we complete our string of four meets with our last easy race, a double dual with Shore Regional and Keyport at home. When the boys stretch, I run the course myself to check for hunters and who knows what else. All clear. Ryan shows a small spark, improving his time on the airport paths by 21 seconds from the last home meet sixteen days before. All of the boys run better and in fact Ryan makes the smallest improvement and finishes fourth, so I don't congratulate myself yet. Brock wins with a 50-second improvement. Two Shore runners beat Ryan. Dunn improves by 63 seconds, Gallagher by 35, and Solebello by 73 as they place 5-6-7 in close order. This is evidence that our training is working and the athletes, at least most of them, are getting tougher. Our spread from Brock to Solebello, our first to fifth and last scorer, is 52 seconds, showing excellent team running. I feel I can train them harder.

It's a Thursday and the boys know we're having a rare Saturday practice at Holmdel. Justin tells me he can't make it because he's going to a Friday-night concert and won't be home till three in the morning. Considering Gallagher's out-of-school crowd and the recent incident, I balk at this and tell him that he'd better show up. Fortunately, Larry Gallagher is here. He left work to help with meet scoring and check on his son. Within minutes, father and son tell me together that Justin is skipping the concert, he'll do his regular busboy job at a local banquet hall, and I'll see him Saturday morning.

I congratulate myself for that one.

Saturday practice has a lighter feel, like a holiday. The boys arrive on time by nine. They're yawning and working the sleep out of their eyes. Other teams show up for the same purpose: a last look at Holmdel before the Monmouth County meet on Tuesday. "We're not running hard today, are we, Coach?" says Dunn. I could have predicted that. I ignore him. Solebello answers for me. "That's why we're here, right, Coach?"

"Hardest practice of the season," I tell them. I want them alert. "You're ready to run harder." I think they all like knowing that, Dunn included.

I try to make it fun. During our strides, I ride their speed relentlessly. "Gallagher, your legs are glued to the ground." "Dunn, c'mon, you're not in the seventh grade anymore. Run with authority." "Brock, you're in slow motion, you couldn't beat the girls' team." I get smart-aleck answers but they run faster. It's a little game we play, the best part of practice because we laugh, and whenever one of the boys really lets loose with a sprint I think these guys seem always to be holding back, even a little, for some male reason I just do not understand.

I'm an archeologist, forever digging. Trying to excavate Gallagher's fierceness.

Time for the real running. My menu: Run the freshman course, run again from the start into the woods, do two short loops in the woods, repeat the freshman course, about six miles of hills total. I get a few fake moans. They do it, and they do it hard. Everyone runs with authority. Maybe it's Saturday, maybe it's our relaxed demeanor or the other teams in our midst. This is not only our hardest practice but also our best. Every boy is strong and sharp and I tell them so.

Solebello asks how I think we'll do in the county meet and I say we have an outside shot at the top five. I remind the boys that if we run to our potential, it'll show we really are state contenders in our division. We talk about Bishop Eustace and Montclair Kimberley, our chief state Parochial B opponents. From the results we've seen, both teams are improving as we are. And the Swede's been running up a storm. The *Star-Ledger* says Nordenbring is one of the best young runners in the state. Montclair has a second boy who's good. He's the nephew of a former cross-country star I remember from my youth. We'll have our hands full.

I scour my files for the latest results from the papers, which I clip like sales coupons. I list contenders for the county and state, including Rumson-Fair Haven, our last dual-meet opponent. I set up charts, use blue, black, green and red pens. I add up the best times of various teams and look at how we'd stack up if we: (a) run okay, (b) run great, (c) bomb out. I'm optimistic, always feeling we'll do great, feeling in my gut that one boy—finally, Lavender?—will rise to the front like, *No problem, Coach, I've had this thing figured out all along.*

I calculate that we can make the top six or seven in Monmouth County, probably the toughest county in the state, led of course by CBA. If we screw up, we'll be in the middle of the twenty-six teams. Last year, we placed seventeenth. Lavender finished twentieth in his best time, 17:22, good for a sophomore but slower than he should have run. He has yet to match that this season. John Lennon was our fourth scorer. If we had Lennon now, I could breathe easier.

I savor my color-coded stats, which take me back to my youth when I was living in Brooklyn and compiled the first high school track performance listings for New York State. I published yearbooks that I sold for a dollar and then two. I loved the look of those gleaming lists of the fastest milers or indoor 600-yard runners or

cross-country performers at Van Cortlandt Park. I gained a reputation and started writing athlete profiles for *Track & Field News*,
which paid me with a free subscription.

Though I favored track and cross-country, I was then drawn to
all sports; friends called me "the encyclopedia." I could recite the
starting lineups of all sixteen major-league baseball clubs. I knew
who held the all-time record for doubles. My father took me to
Ebbets Field to watch the Dodgers and one time we had box seats
for a twilight doubleheader with the Reds and I could see Ted
Kluszewski's thick arms close up. When the Mets started, I was a
New York Post contest winner in predicting the Mets' starting lineup and got a baseball with the players' signatures, which gradually
wore off as friends came into my bedroom and handled the prize
ball I had on display.

In high school I worshiped the neighborhood star, Rico
Petrocelli, who went on to play for the Red Sox. When I ran track
and found my efforts unsatisfying, I focused on my teammates'
performances, which almost got me thrown off the team. One year
at the Penn Relays, I conducted a team pool, twenty-five cents a
man, in predicting the times of our relay runners. The coach didn't
like the idea of a boy knowing his teammates bet he would run
poorly. He threatened me with expulsion, so I directed my energies
into a more positive vein, organizing a team donation to the U.S.
Olympic Committee to help our 1964 Olympic team at Tokyo.
When Billy Mills was the upset winner of the games in the 10,000
meters, I was sure our ten-dollar donation had made the difference.

All along I hoped I would one day coach, and now my boys' stats
tickle me with the satisfaction that I have taken them from ungain-
ly freshmen in their first summer practices to contenders in their
junior season in the county and beyond. If the boys are finally all

running with authority, I feel I am coaching with authority. Their success clarifies for me what I am doing: passing on a tradition that has meaning in every aspect of life. After Ron Delany of Ireland won the 1956 Olympic 1500 meters in Melbourne, he fell to the ground and the bronze medalist, John Landy, thought Delany was hurt. Delany said he was praying thanks, not for the gold medal but for what running had given him.

I feel the St. Rose boys are ready for that in our final, climactic weeks. For the opportunity to say thanks for what running has given us. We can do it with how we run, and with how we appreciate it.

I think again of the theologian Aquinas, who combined faith with reason. My boys could not have come this far on reason alone. They faced too many hurdles, and the devil was always there (in our case, the sea) to offer an easy way out. Faith has smiled on me and my boys. In our belief, we have created a new reality.

No one can remember a more beautiful season of running. At the county meet, it's sixty degrees, sunny, no wind. The foliage at Holmdel is at its peak. The trails are lush with reds and yellows and the scene, gazing from the woods down toward the start, with the opening ascent flanked by trees and the duck pond in the background, is like a Thomas Cole painting.

It's a day for a runner to shine. A no-excuses day when you're in late-season shape with over five hundred miles in your legs and a dozen races under your belt. Just follow your heart, listen to the coach, go to the bathroom before the line grows too long, and you'll do fine.

I try to be low-key. I don't want to make too much of the county meet because this is not what our season hinges on. I will save my big command for state. Brock has a cold and coughs up some gook but I minimize it. Still, it's hard not to be souped up after the sizable preview in the *Asbury Park Press*, which ballyhoos CBA, enviously referred to by my fellow coaches as "University of Lincroft."

The park fills with dads in business suits who rushed over from Lucent and moms with small children in their arms and retirees who set up beach chairs near the start and tilt their heads toward the sunshine. Cameras click and hum. Little kids munch fast food from the concession stand as their older brothers and sisters take their last sips of water, remove all jewelry, pat their hair, blow their noses, and secure their belongings before taking the starting line.

The boys gather closely to pray before I can remind them to, and when they do I feel their awesome power. How manly they seem now, and I marvel at how they confront the race, lacking fear or at least not showing it, ready to do one of the toughest things asked of young athletes. Perhaps they feel a holy will, finally poised to fulfill a command of their religious tradition, as explained to me by Bob Andrews, longtime coach of Archbishop Molloy High in Queens and a former clergyman, who said:

"A distance runner is in one sense alone. He is left to think, to meditate, to answer questions from within. In the Catholic tradition there's a lot of talk about the will of the Father. In cross-country, there's a time when a young boy becomes committed and wants to see that will played out."

From the opening strides, St. Rose is in there, in the race for the top spots, their purple jerseys mixing with those of the big names in the field of 183. The CBA kids come flying by and Brock and Ryan are in the second tier, lifting themselves over the first, biting hill and into the flow of the race. Brock is not conceding anything. Ryan is not being rash. They're right where they should be. I yell for them with words they will recognize: "Perfect position, stick together, this is your day . . ." Dunn, Gallagher and Solebello appear next with only seconds between them. There is not a weak brow among them.

I fly to the checkpoints—the Bowl, tennis courts, and mouth of the last wooded section leading to the finish. Same strides, same faces for my boys, positioned close with every good team but CBA. The five of them work the downhills and come out into the open fiercely, doing the right thing by not looking back, only ahead, grinding to the finish. They don't pick up any places but they don't lose any. We're light on short speed and need to work on that. No one unleashes a sprint but they muscle across the line proudly like they belong.

Brock is seventeenth in 17:22, his best time by 10 seconds despite his cold. Ryan is twenty-eighth in 17:38, his best time this season. Mike Dunn is fortieth in 17:58, his best time by 28 seconds and first time breaking 18:00. Gallagher is forty-fourth in 18:06, his best time by 12 seconds. Mike Solebello is sixty-fourth in 18:22, his best time by 13 seconds. Chris Ruhl, our sixth man, gets a huge personal best in 19:54, his first time under 20:00, and John Leschak, finally eluding detention, runs 21:27 for his best performance.

St. Rose places fifth with 193 points among twenty-six teams. The CBA Colts score 26 and are entitled to keep their noses in the air. Middletown South (140), Holmdel (166), and St. John Vianney (190) are second, third, and fourth, and with my boys close on their heels we feel part of the day's conversation. Our five-man scoring average is 17:53, which should make Bishop Eustace and Montclair Kimberley take notice. Only nine points behind us in sixth is Rumson-Fair Haven, setting up an exciting dual-meet showdown for the Class B Central division title next week.

I give hugs all around and embrace parents and tell the boys, there, you did it, you showed what you're made of, doesn't it feel great? They don't have to answer. Only Solebello does. "I feel great, Coach," he says. "I think I'm ready to break eighteen." I tell him if he breaks eighteen the state meet is ours. But I sound a cautionary note. First we have Rumson to run on our home course. It's the course more than Rumson that worries me. A twisted ankle—or snakebite—at the airport swamp is the last thing we need.

We leave in a celebratory mood and I announce another Saturday practice to prepare for Rumson. On the home course and I'll bring breakfast. Before that, we finish the week at the lake and boardwalk with easy mileage and a ladder workout in which the boys repeat sets of thirty-second, sixty-second, and ninety-second runs, interspersed with equal rest-jogs. No one lags. Leschak tries to keep up with the leaders and does briefly until folding his tent and having to walk.

Empowered, the boys sit silently on the boardwalk pavilion with eyes closed for visualization training. They requested it. I notice a couple of smiles in their repose. I hold them for a count of sixty. I ask if anyone minds sharing his image. Then, I say no, keep them to yourselves. They need private moments. It's those secrets that get to me.

The wind kicks up on the beach as I grab the boys one by one for individual assessment. It's my midseason sit-down three weeks late. We sit off to the side. I look each boy in the eye and ask: How do you feel about your season, what can I do to help you run even better? Before we're done I reinforce what's expected of them for the remaining meets and the state finale.

Brock's pleased with his running and wants to train harder. I tell him I know he can trainer harder but we have to be careful to avoid injury, especially at this pivotal point. I remind him he's got to stay number one and lead the team.

Ryan's not pleased with his running and says it's not his family; that's working out, that's not a problem, he doesn't know why he's not doing better. I tell him, focus on the running, clear your head, show you can overcome anything and rise to the top. I get the gold medal for platitudes but that's all I can come up with right now. I tell him he should be up with Brock so it's simple: Stick with Brock and if possible find the power to surpass him.

Mike Dunn turns quiet when not in the group and I have to draw him out. I tell him he showed the true Michael with his county race and can run another thirty seconds better. No doubt about it. Trust yourself, I tell him.

Justin's running, I gradually learn, is a miracle, according to some of the guys, who tell me he has a way of finding trouble, or is it that trouble finds him? He's reticent. Repeat your county run, that's all you have to do. Repeat your county run. Everything okay? Yep.

Mike Solebello's loving his running, his new best times, his distance ability as a sprinter, and his fishing and hunting expeditions. I tell him there's no turning back now. He's a cross-country runner, at least part of the year, so feel part of the group, don't sell yourself short.

Chris never thought he'd hold up through four seasons of cross-country so everything he achieves is gravy. He's improved every meet this fall and I tell him, don't forget you're a key member of the varsity, our sixth man, if anyone has a bad race you move up to a scorer and could affect the outcome. He nods his head yes like I've just sent him off to war.

Leschak—whom I never call John but Leschak because he deserves single-name status like, say, Kafka—says that, yes, he will do me a huge personal favor and avoid getting a detention the rest of the season so I don't have to plead with the athletic director in vain for special dispensation. Wear a tie, button your shirt, keep your mouth shut, whatever it takes. No problem, Coach.

No problem, Coach. I've come this far, so very far, the coach of these grand kids. I have them in my grasp. They have me in their grasp. We're in this together, me and my boys, as never before, and I can't let go, not an inch, and people around me know that and give me my space, whether or not they understand. My wife, Andrea, tries to understand, but when I don't accompany her to an important doctor's appointment because of practice, my coaching takes a whipping it deserves, though I won't admit it.

I will admit I need a break and we head down to Washington to visit our younger daughter at college. Being with Jamie reminds me of how needy I can be. Her kindness and sensitivity are too much to take lightly. We walk hand in hand on campus. I don't want to let go and when it's time to leave I feel a void I thought I'd learned to conquer. My emotions are stretched as I hold Jamie's sweetness in my bosom, listen to my wife's pleas to keep the team in perspective, and check in with my father to see if the nurses answered his late-night call to help him go to the bathroom.

9

Fight to the Finish

On the last Saturday in October, the St. Rose cross-country grounds are as barren as a cornfield in winter. The soccer and field hockey teams are elsewhere and the greens are whipped by howling winds that topple the makeshift breakfast I've set up for the boys on a small snack table. I've laid out bagels and cream cheese, peanut butter and jelly, orange juice and water. The napkins and paper plates fly madly and the boys dart around in circles grabbing what they can. Everyone's present except Michael Dunn. That pisses me off. Missing a critical practice at this point. Later he tells me he slept at a friend's house and could not get a train back and then a ride over. Sounds plausible but I'm still pissed. Everything must be right for the Rumson-Fair Haven meet.

Rumson is why I risked getting flak at school for skipping today's Catholic Track Conference meet, considered an obligation. With two divisions based on enrollment, CBA was a lock to win the CTC A race, while we were favored in B. But the trophy would be meaningless if we compromised our readiness against Rumson in three days with the dual-meet title on the line. When I explained to athletic people at school that we'd already competed too much, they said we'd blown a big victory and chattered like I didn't know what I was doing.

You can't explain running to some people. What the boys need this Saturday is practice specifically geared to the kind of race we can expect out of Rumson, a team we face for the first time in our new divisional alignment this season. The towns of Rumson and Fair Haven are two of the wealthiest in the state, with Rumson known for its breathtaking estates on the Navesink River. But the Rumson boys are no elitists. They compete with a savvy blue-collar style. They are mostly seniors and use their experience, and muscle, to win.

Rumson is 6-0. St. Rose is 6-0. The winner will be Class B Central champions.

With Rumson only nine points behind us in the county meet, the two teams are evenly matched. Rumson's collective race times are virtually the equal of ours. Whichever team runs a perfectly executed race will prevail. That boils down to two things: smart, patient pacing for the first 2.5 miles through the woods, then a hard, gutsy drive on the flat, grassy stretch to the finish.

Each runner will count as never before. This race—team vs. team, man vs. man—will be the essence of running. It will take everything we know, every morsel of energy, every ounce of fight, and probably a bit of luck. It's the most significant race the boys have been dealt and an ideal lead-in to the state meet eleven days later. Run well and we'll be ready for state. Mess up and our hopes could slip away.

Competing at home against Rumson should give us a slight advantage. But we can't be complacent about that. The Rumson kids are older, wiser, and bigger. They have one boy over six feet with a stride as long as the Swede's. Last year, when Mater Dei beat us for the title, the loss came at home.

The boys secure the food platters with stones as we prepare to run. I have them do their warm-up in the woods and I jog over when they're done. As the boys stretch on a dirt patch near the new airport hangar, they seem anxious. I tell them just run like you did in the county meet and we'll do fine.

But they understand there's a big difference now. The county meet was a showcase but there was little at stake. Now it's Us vs. Them with everything at stake. I don't soften the challenge. I tell the boys this is the test we've been waiting for. And how fortunate we are that Rumson is a worthy opponent and not an easy mark. It will—would—make our victory that much sweeter. The Class B Central title carries honor.

I point to the woods where we run two loops and say, "Let them lead. We know the course, we know the rhythm, the heavy, sandy spots, where to make moves . . ."

Then I stop. I'm planting seeds. The race plan will be outlined on Tuesday. My words are intended for Brock and Ryan. The rest of the team will receive different instructions. This is not a race I can be cute about and just let happen. I must be an effective game coach. I have to rally the boys with pinpoint precision. We know a lot. We must deal with our smart bombs.

"Coach," says Brock, "what if Rumson decides to do the same thing? What if they plan to follow *us*?"

Brilliant. "I don't think they will," I say. "They're aggressive. They like to lead. I think they'll take the race to us on our home course."

I explain our workout. "The race will probably come down to the last stretch when we run through the gate and race for the finish. Whoever pushes more, tries harder, runs through pain, will win.

Today we're going to run five repeats, 600s, from the gate to the tape. This will not only make you stronger but also add to your confidence in your kick. When you run on Tuesday, recall your runs on this section and gather all your power."

The boys embrace the workout, seizing the Rumson meeting with carnivorous glee. They proceed to run like they own the place. Just what I'd hoped. Brock and Ryan take turns at the front. Mike Solebello's speed over this short distance puts him right up there. The boys do their reps in a little more than a minute and a half. I give them a minute's jog-rest. They do it again, and again, five in all. After each run, we check pulse rates. They're nice and low after a brief rest. The boys' expressions, almost arrogant, ask for more.

The contour of today's path is half a rectangle. A right turn through the gate from the woods, then two hard lefts around the soccer field, a curve around the baseball backstop, and a soft left to the home straight for the finish. The wind propels the boys when they start, then hits them squarely after the last turn, as though they've come out from behind a building. Lavender's lush hair flows back. Leschak's gelled stalks don't budge.

I work the practice like I will the meet. Affirmative calls, broad gestures, close-up orders. "Outstanding. This is your day. Tuesday will be your day. Solebello, best practice ever. Perfect. Perfect. We're all set. I love it. Gallagher, stick with it. Patience, Leschak, patience. Run your pace. Smart and strong. Smart and strong. The wind is your friend. Break through the wall. You know you can. Attaboy, you've done it . . ."

The boys sweat up the morning and it's a clean runner's sweat—"the sweat of honest toil," as Roger Bannister once put it. Afterward, the boys chat up the meet. For the first time, at least that I've heard, they encourage each other. Brock applauds Mike, and Mike applauds Brock. The comments are instructive, too, with specific advice for Tuesday. I've said enough and listen. We munch on bagels and kid around and I want to hold on to the moment, one of great anticipation. The gulf between teacher and student has shrunk to almost nothing. But the guys eat quickly and take off.

Suddenly, I'm alone at the field. The sun hides and the wind grows cold. I clean up the breakfast, lock the gates, and head on home thinking it's Saturday in the village, the best time of all.

On Tuesday, we depart for the meet from St. Rose in the same formation as always. Chris Ruhl, the senior, drives Gallagher, Dunn, and Silvestri. I take Lavender, Solebello, and Leschak. Lavender always hangs with Leschak. Lavender, more than the others, understands Leschak's outer limits and enjoys the idea of protecting Leschak from himself, should the need arise. The boys wear sweatshirts and windbreakers in the cool weather. Leschak wears a T-shirt and jewelry.

When we get to the field, Rumson is already there. That's a first. Usually we have a long wait for the opposing team to show up. Meet officials hate that because they want to start early and leave. Rumson's waiting for *us*. Rumson parents are here. The St. Rose athletic director, Dick Alger, is here, and he rarely takes in a cross-country meet. The school trainer, the lovely Melinda, is here, as are runners' friends from school who never come but know this could be a race for all time.

"I'm nervous, Coach," says Solebello as we prepare for the warm-up.

I tell everyone that a little nervousness is good. It shows you care, you want to race and do your best. Being nervous will pump you up and get your system activated, and most runners would rather feel a little nervous than totally relaxed. The musician Miles Davis said if you're not nervous you're not paying attention.

The boys buzz. Lavender looks intent but says nothing. That worries me.

I steer Solebello away from the race by bringing up the fishing trip he'd told me his marine biology class took. He talks about his catch. That calms him. It also calms me. If the boys are nervous, I have to be a stabilizing influence. I have to look confident and cool like everything's going to happen the way we want.

But when we usher the Rumson boys to the woods to see the course as part of both teams' warm-up, my coolness is put to a jarring test. Rumson seems to know the course all too well. I hear that two days ago, on Sunday, they practiced here, too. Then, midway along on a sandy section, Lavender stops and walks. Shoe loose? He walks a good twenty or thirty seconds examining one portion of the path like a surveyor. When I ask Ryan what's up, he says "I'm just looking it over," but I'm not close to him so his words are unclear and I'm not sure if he also says something like "this is where I'll make my move."

I stand there stunned. I don't want to squelch initiative. I've worked three years with these boys to get them to this point of caring how they run and approaching a race with calculation and integrity. Lavender has evidently been thinking and has a plan. But is it in sync with my plan? I decide to let him be. There is latitude in every race. I want to trust Lavender's instincts. In recent meets he has quelled his tendency to shoot ahead recklessly.

We run to rejoin the group, finish the woods inspection, and get ready to take the start. I kneel down with the boys around me and review our strategy. I look each boy in the eye. I remind Ryan and Brock to let Rumson lead. "Let them do the work, let them think they're in control. Then, on the second of the two loops in the woods, where the sand gets heavy on an ascent, surge ahead and

carry your strength all the way home. If you pace yourself properly, you should have enough in reserve to move ahead and hold it.
And you'll catch Rumson by surprise." I pause and repeat emphat-
ically, "There's absolutely no benefit in leading early. It can only hurt
you in the end."

Brock and Ryan nod.

Rumson's top three boys, Jon Irwin, Joe Clabby, and Chris
Rumpf, have shown themselves to be slightly better than us man
for man. In the county meet, they ran 16:59, 17:21, and 17:31.
Brock, Ryan and Mike Dunn ran 17:22, 17:38, and 17:58. Our
fourth and fifth scorers, however, are superior to Rumson's, who
ran 18:16, and 18:55 at county. Gallagher and Solebello ran 18:06
and 18:22. I tell Brock and Ryan they must break up the Rumson
front three by allowing no more than one Rumson boy to outrun
them. I play down the individual victory; that's irrelevant.

"You two," I say to Brock and Ryan. "You two have to finish no
worse than second and third."

"Mike Dunn, keep the front group in sight. If you can run with
Rumson's third guy, fine. If not, just protect sixth place. Do not let
another Rumson boy beat you . . ." I pause for effect. "Run with
authority.

"Gallagher and Solebello, you guys keep Dunn in sight if you
can. Your job is to make sure you're ahead of Rumson's fourth and
fifth guys. You beat them handily at Holmdel, you'll beat them
again."

Before they recite the "Hail Mary," I ask everyone to touch hands
in the middle of our circle. "If we do what we're capable of, if we run
smart and strong the way we're supposed to, we should run 2-3-6-
7-8 if not better. Then we'll win, 26-29."

I don't also say we can run 2-4-6-7-8 and still win, 27-28. That scenario suggests Ryan would be fourth, and I don't want him to think that's okay. He's got to aim for third or better. He and Brock 2-3, that's the deal. I have no doubt we can do it. Even though Rumson has the edge on paper, I think my boys are hungrier and indeed we are at home, where, by now, the quirky contours of the course should be to our liking.

I tell the boys one last thing before I give them up to the race. "Just do your best and I'll be proud of you."

The official grows impatient and hurries us to the line. He alternates Rumson and St. Rose, boys right, girls left. Everyone starts together. Karen Lavender has the ice cream sticks to hand to finishers. Sue Solebello has my clipboard for scoring and her husband, Mike, has my stopwatch around his neck to call off times. I want to be free to roam the course.

The starter waits for stillness, raises his arm skyward, and shoots the pistol. I cut to the gate where the boys will enter the woods and wonder if I've told them enough. At these moments, I want to lay out everything I know about running and the impulses that enable a runner to fly. But the boys are supposed to take more responsibility for their success. They usually show me they know more than I realize. It's time for more of their secrets to reveal themselves.

"Pop-pop." Waiting with the Rumson coach, Warren Brown, and parents from both teams, we hear cracks that sound like gunshots. Hunters' gunshots. But here come the boys . . .

Brock and Ryan stick together with the three Rumson guys. Good, good. Everything's good. Dunn, Gallagher, and Solebello are close behind, ahead of the Rumson runners they must beat. I deliver my calls, not that loud, just so they hear my voice. Brown, who's been coaching longer than I, says little.

The runners go off on the first loop. I wait anxiously, making small talk with Brown. I hope I soon see the same formation with the loop completed: Rumson leading with Brock and Ryan close and holding back. I'm confident I will.

But I don't. Lavender's ahead. He's got ten, fifteen yards. He's going for it. He must have bolted where he stopped on the warmup. Shit. My optimism fades to fear. Brock is positioned perfectly with the Rumson trio but now has to battle them alone, and he's clearly outnumbered against athletes with sharp elbows. My other boys look good. But Ryan is out there exposed, where he's been too often before and blown it, and I don't have good reason to think he can hold on and steal the race. If he does, he's a hero but a superficial one—getting the right result with the wrong act. If he fades, he'll be hurt and we'll all feel let down, a crushing and perhaps irreconcilable blow with the state meet around the corner.

All I can do is pace, check my watch, and kiss my mezuzah like I did for Leschak when he needed help from a higher power. But Leschak welcomed help. Ryan seems stuck on going it alone even if it destroys him.

The boys' positions after the second loop will set them up for the drive to the finish. Who's tapped out? Who's got something left? I stare down the sandy path pleading for Lavender's hair.

I pick out Rumson instead. It's Clabby, the six-footer. He's comes up the ascent first with a teammate second, Brock third and not giving up, Rumson also fourth, and Ryan fifth, looking haggard. Dunn, Gallagher, and Solebello have six, seven, and eight all but sewn up. The race will be decided out front, where it should be, as the field moves back into the open, and the boys have a minute-and-change to affect their lives in ways they will not soon forget.

I scream like there's no tomorrow. About pumping your arms, looking ahead, no glancing back, pushing. About catching the guy ahead, not giving up on yourself. With great force in his shoulders, Brock powers ahead of the second Rumson man, Irwin, and goes after Clabby. If Brock beats Clabby, even with Ryan still fifth and lacking fight, we'll win. But that's too much to ask. Brock has come through bravely and that's how it stands: Rumson 1-3-4-9-10 for 27, St. Rose 2-5-6-7-8 for 28.

One point. Ryan didn't have to be third. He could have been fourth. He tried to be first and wound up fifth. Too many truths for one afternoon. What am I going to do with Ryan?

I recall the "Julio" story I wrote in 1986 when I interviewed the Boys High coach, Doug Terry, about why his favored team wound up in a photo-finish defeat against Andrew Jackson High. He said he realized it was because his best runner, the superior anchorman Jim Jackson, personalized the race, using it as revenge against the Jackson anchor, Mark Ferrell, who'd upset him the previous week in the city championships. Terry told me that as a coach you have to be able to assess when an athlete chooses to isolate a goal that diverges from the team's. "Jack was personally after Mark Ferrell," Terry said. "I was after the record. That's when we lost each other."

Ryan was personally after . . . what? The glory of victory? Fact is, he was probably capable of winning. But then we enter the murky thesis of whether he could handle victory, and the pressure of being our top runner going into the state meet. Taking the lead against Rumson was perhaps a Ryan tease: showing the talent, as I'd suggested at the Hudson meet, but not committing to it. Or could it be like the defiant young lad in *The Loneliness of the Long-Distance Runner*: showing he could win but rejecting establishment values by stopping? In Ryan's case, I suppose his parents—or could it be me?—would be the object of his scorn.

My boys walk around, barely able to keep their spent bodies

upright, in the daze of defeat. Clabby's winning time is 15:25. Brock ran 15:29, his best. Sweat covers him and Brock looks like every great runner I've seen after a successful race: assured, content, wanting more.

Lavender's time is 15:49. Dunn, Solebello, and Gallagher ran 16:08, 16:21 and 16:30; they did their jobs. Chris Ruhl improved another fifty-seven seconds to 17:15, and he's closing in on the top five. Leschak, running 18:17, made the biggest improvement of all.

There are handshakes all around and talk that we're all winners today but we don't accept that. It's clear that Lavender's immature act blew it for us, and for him. *Do your best and I'll be proud of you.* This is not Ryan's best, dammit! I thought we'd put his impulsiveness behind us. This lapse in judgment must be confronted here and now. I can't let the boys think I'm going to let it pass. I owe the team a dressing-down of Ryan. I owe it to Ryan. But I can't let him feel crushed by the team's censure with the state meet coming up. We've come too far to retreat. I cannot let the demons manipulating Ryan's psyche get any darker. The boy just has to know he did wrong.

The team does my work for me. First, Brock complains that when he was running with the three Rumson boys they were clipping him, knocking him off-stride. With Ryan ahead, Brock was a lone soldier among the enemy. Brock's point is, this aggression was unfair and also that he could have used some help in the trenches. I say that maybe it was unfair but if someone shaves you like that you have to hold your ground and reciprocate or they'll take advantage. Ryan's teeth clench with anger. He seems focused not on his mistake but on Rumson's heavy-handed style. I don't realize how Ryan takes my words of combat to heart.

Solebello, visibly upset, blurts out, "What about Ryan taking the lead like that, Coach?" I say it was not a very smart move. Ryan looks away. That's enough for now. The boys gobble up the tray of homemade brownies Brock's mom brought. Tomorrow is a Catholic holiday so we'll all have a day to cool out. Of course, I tell the boys to run on their own.

I summon Melinda to take me back into the woods in her golf cart to retrieve the cones I'd set up marking the course. Dick Alger supervises a total cleanup since all fall teams using the field have now finished home events. It's dusk as I depart with Ryan in my craw and I think I'm not such a model team player, either, since I've passed up today's important family meeting with the therapists at Dad's rehab center. My brother spends his days checking on Dad's progress. I admit my shortcoming: I have to be with my boys.

Back on the boardwalk for practice, the boys pick up the pieces of the Rumson meet but without ill will. There are still cars and girls and fishing to talk about. I can't let it go that easily. I want to talk more with Ryan but don't. I speak with his parents. Ryan's schoolwork seems okay. He's got the girlfriend, that's good. I think there's no way to make divorce easy, and Ryan's going to have to get through it.

I think about Rumson's roughhouse tactics and berate myself for not making more of that factor before the meet. It should have been obvious, like the mud in North Carolina. I didn't coach the obvious. Maybe I could have coaxed Ryan to remain at Brock's side during combat. In my zeal to coach pure running, I'm forgetting about the outside forces, whether they're natural or man-made. I'm going for theory at the expense of pragmatism. Tom Heath of the University of Lincroft would never let that happen.

As the boys jog around the lake, I stare out to the sea as another day of sun-drenched beauty blankets the Shore. Summer at the beach was always the happiest time for me growing up. Every season in Brooklyn we went to Brighton Beach Baths, where the women would serve food secured in vault-like containers and the men would play cards. I spent hours in the pool or out on the beach with my friends and always avoided trouble from older boys who would kick you off the basketball court or push you around for no reason. I marveled at how my best friend Evan would take on bigger kids in a fight, which usually came about over some careless remark made by his younger brother Stevie. I can picture one encounter, bare knuckles, that had Evan launching into a guy's face from a fighter's crouch. Me, I would have probably called my mother.

So the notion of boys being hostile in cross-country, in which a charitable ethos rules, doesn't quite register in my genes. Perhaps my instruction to the team should have been, "Let them lead and at the right moment run right through them." But I guess I'm just not a kick-ass coach.

I let the delicious day at the beach inhabit me. I envy shore residents who seem on permanent vacation. Many of those I come in contact with, the senior citizens bundled in chaise lounges getting their last licks of the sun, are long since retired. The serenity brings me down to earth and I remind myself how nice it is, still, to hear the boys call me "Coach."

Even when Michael Dunn says, "Coach, I'm quitting."

Or when I ask Brock how he thought he ran against Rumson and he says, "Good, Coach."

Or when Mike Solebello switches the boys' conversation about the cars they'll drive when they get their licenses to say, "Coach, you notice any differences in us from freshman year to now?"

When I respond that they've grown in every way from pathetic little shrimps into maturing young men, the boys launch into a debate over who was the most pathetic and shrimpiest and all the screwy things they did as freshmen. Solebello says he recently looked at the freshman team book and saw how puny and unathletic they all looked. Solebello's proud of what he and his teammates have accomplished, and it's clear that a one-point loss to Rumson, no matter how distasteful, is not going to change that. Good to know.

The time-line discussion brings up questions about next season. "Coach, what's the schedule for next summer?" "Coach, are we going back to North Carolina?" Lavender, who's been quiet, perks up and says he's got certain goals for the winter track season and would like to attend a running camp for a week next summer. I encourage that, saying it would be great if the whole team could attend a camp as some teams do, but I wish Lavender would address what's currently on the table.

I wonder if Ryan's problem stems in part from the instantaneous pleasures of our high-tech life. The tendency to seek satisfaction without responsibility. Push a key and everything you need is right in front of your nose. Race ahead without considering the consequences. The culture of speed. *No time to wait. I want it now.* I thought I'd coached immediate gratification out of the boys. Maybe six out of seven isn't so bad.

We have a race on Saturday, the Shore Conference meet, the last one before state. But it's a throwaway for us. It's the one meet all season for which I tell the boys, just run how you feel, it's not important where you place, check out Holmdel in a meet situation one more time before state. Today's workout is hard because we don't need to be rested for Saturday. We're putting more speed in our legs for state.

We do five sets of 30-45-60 around the lake. Run thirty seconds fast, thirty seconds slow, forty-five fast, forty-five slow, sixty fast, sixty slow. That's fifteen sprints, more intensity than they're used to. The workout is designed to fortify their kick for the final straight-away at state. Solebello questions why I change the time from thirty to forty-five to sixty. Why not repeat the same time so they can maintain a steady rhythm? I explain that they need to learn to change rhythm to cover surges made by opponents in a race.

At Holmdel, before the Shore Conference meet, I pull Ryan aside. The other guys have gone to the finish to watch the girls' race so we're alone.

"Why did you take the lead against Rumson? What did you hope to accomplish?"

"The pace was slow, like they were walking," he says. "I had to do something. It was our home course."

Foolish pride. "If the pace felt slow, all the better, you'll have energy to burn when it counts. Save it, use it to your advantage later on, don't set yourself up, don't do the other team a favor by leading early. Being impulsive, in running or anything else, does not get you what you want."

Ryan defends his act, saying he just couldn't stand to wait any longer. I remind him how it turned out: that he only needed to out-run one of Rumson's top three, but they all beat him and that's why we lost. Finally, he says okay, maybe he should have waited to surge on the second loop. But I think he just wants to get rid of me. We finish on good terms but Ryan's disposition makes me uneasy.

Moments later, Ryan rushes behind a clump of bushes and vomits. A cynic on the team says, "Oh, he's sick or something." I think, *Yeah, great excuse for not running well.* Dennis Lavender is here. I look at him and we both sort of shrug. When I approach Ryan, he says he wasn't feeling that good but now he's fine.

The Shore Conference boys' varsity race has more than two hundred runners, the largest single field all season at Holmdel. As the boys crest the opening hill, Brock is up around twelfth, running over his head, and I doubt he can hold it. But Brock is smart enough to know that this is a race in which to experiment, gamble, try things that could be used at state. Maybe start out faster or key off one of the better CBA guys. Or keep clear of the logjam that follows as thick knots of runners compete shoulder to shoulder for space on the narrow path following the hill.

Brock is ahead of all the Rumson boys. Mike Dunn comes next for St. Rose. He finds clear footing for his thin frame. Then comes Ryan. He's boxed in and looks agitated. I'm positioned as always on the road for cars a few feet from the trail. I can see Ryan's frustration. He's cornered with no room to move. His stride is compressed. But it's only temporary. The whole race remains. Be patient and when space opens up down the trail you can fly.

Suddenly, a runner whom I don't recognize until later on as being from Rumson gives Ryan a shoulder block, knocking him off-stride and practically off the course. I don't see it as intentional. There's a lot of jostling in the dense pack. A shove like this will occur ten times during the race. It happens.

Ryan becomes enraged. He gets back in the race and goes after the kid, who is now about twenty yards ahead of him. Okay, I think, let Ryan run rings around him if he can. Ryan does not run past the Rumson boy. Instead he runs up his back and pushes him off-balance. The kid tilts but doesn't fall, turns around and throws a punch at Ryan, grazing his face, drawing blood. Ryan, startled, swings at the boy, and they exchange furious blows. Then, as though nothing happened, the two of them resume running and Ryan sprints ahead, fueled by adrenaline.

I am aghast. Horrified. Mortified. Petrified. I shit in my pants. I feel assaulted. Violated. Confused. This is the beauty of cross-country I've been raving about? The path toward righteousness? I haven't felt such alarm since the summer in the sixties when I worked as a waiter at a Catskills hotel and a kitchen worker bunked in the room next to mine knifed someone in the middle of the night. I shit in my pants then, too.

In my day, cross-country was a pacifist's art. Body contact was anathema. We were so pure many thought winning was beside the point. Lead runners would hold hands across the finish trying to tie and show solidarity. Intentional ties were against the rules, and there were disqualifications. When elite runners starting doing it, they were too big to be bounced. I remember Frank Shorter, the 1972 Olympic marathon champion, finishing hand in hand with Jack Bacheler, another '72 Olympic marathoner whom Shorter considered a mentor.

While I've seen a few skirmishes in track, I'd never seen a fight in cross-country. All the life drained out of me as I watched the encounter. The fear that struck me was primarily for Ryan and the depth of his apparent victimhood. Experts believe that children of divorce feel like victims. They have no power to control the events swirling around them. Cross-country is Ryan's turf, the one place where, if threatened, he could exercise power. It seems like he felt, *I'm not going to take it anymore*. If he needed to explode, who could blame him. But here?

Now I've got a fine mess on my hands. Major damage control with Ryan, the rest of the team, the Rumson camp, meet officials if anyone saw it. The team, or Ryan, could be banned from the state meet. Crazier things have happened. The state association has no truck with stuff like this. St. Rose could suffer an embarrassment.

Could be a lawsuit.

I just want to coach running.

I consider the repercussions as I walk up the course. I'm too shaken to run or make it to the Bowl. The meet itself has become totally irrelevant. A couple of minutes later, I see Ryan. He's stopped. He rips off his race number and walks toward me. Okay, let's hear it. He says the Rumson kid pushed him and shows me his lower leg. He says it's bruised and hurts. He shows me the cut on his face where the kid punched him. He tells me he quit the race because he doesn't want to make his leg worse with the state meet coming up. I tell him we'll talk more after the race, I've got to keep track of the other boys, and I send him back to the start to ice his leg.

With a mile left Brock runs by. He looks awful. His early excitement wasted him. Dunn, too, and Solebello. Everyone looks defeated. That's the kind of day it is. The only bright spot is Leschak, who improves another forty-five seconds and is threatening twenty minutes. His mom is there to see it, which makes me proud. She tells me she's getting fed up with St. Rose for all the detentions John gets for things like the way his belt is buckled. She says she sent her son to a private school for the discipline but this is too much.

If only I had a belt buckle to worry about. Word of the fight gets around the team. Dick Alger sees me and inquires about it. I didn't even know he was at the park. I summarize but protect Ryan and attribute equal blame to his adversary. My mission is to speak with the Rumson coach, get the two boys to shake hands, and be done with it. Then I'll have to deal with my team.

I see Ryan. He says his leg is fine. I knew that.

I find Warren Brown, the Rumson coach. He is unaware of the altercation. I have to be careful. I explain what transpired and tell him I think the boy tangling with Ryan was one of his kids. He's taken aback. The Rumson team has their belongings under a tree only a few yards from where St. Rose is spread out. Brown calls to his boys, who can tell something is up, "Does anyone know anything about this?" Their expressions say they do but no one volunteers a word.

I take it upon myself to address them, saying, "We don't want to blame anybody or get anyone in trouble or disqualified. We just want to get the two guys together, shake hands and forget about it."

The Rumson captain comes forward and goes to find the team slugger, who is cleaning himself up in the bathroom. It's Rumpf, their number three guy who placed fourth in our dual meet, just ahead of Ryan. Brown takes his runner aside and they talk. I do the same with Ryan, who admits he overreacted. Ryan picked the wrong guy to tangle with. Brown tells me later that Rumpf is also on the wrestling team.

"If someone pushes you," I tell Ryan in a punitive but low voice, "you get back in the race and show how tough you are by running the pants off the kid. That's how you respond. If something is done to you that violates the rules, you tell me and I'll determine if any follow-up action is necessary."

Ryan says the boy was the one who pushed Brock in the dual meet. "Doesn't matter," I tell him. "You settle the score by outrunning him."

Brown brings Rumpf over and he and Ryan shake hands. No words or eye contact. Brown and I nod to each other. I hope we can keep this between us.

Ryan's father, Dennis, witnesses the whole thing. He concurs with how I handled the situation and wishes he had a remedy for his son's behavior. We both say how Ryan had better not let this kind of anger boil over to the street, where a handshake won't be a convenient salve. I feel for Dennis, who checks with me regularly on how Ryan is doing. I feel for myself. I don't know if I have the energy to keep the team humming for one more week.

Before leaving the park, the boys grumble about Ryan, who's gone with his father. Solebello says of the scuffle, "That's the wrong thing to do, Coach." He's not asking me. He's telling everyone. I nod my head. I'm too upset to talk.

Later that night, I call Ryan to see how he's doing and make sure he understands his mistake. I tell him he has to put it behind him and go on. One more race this season to show what he's got and help the team. He says no problem, Coach, everything's going to be fine. And I have to rely on that.

The next day, however, Ryan calls me to say that his girlfriend, who runs for Middletown South, said her coach heard that Ryan and the Rumson boy would not be allowed in the state meet because of the fight. Did some official see what took place on Saturday? I call Dick Alger on Monday, the start of our state meet week, and he says no one has notified him of any such thing. By the time I arrive at school for practice, the official paperwork with the team's confirmed state meet roster has arrived.

So Lavender's in. But soon I learn that our lineup may still be in jeopardy.

10

The Genius of Youth

"Coach," says Mike Solebello as I enter St. Rose to gather the boys for practice, "did you hear about Gallagher?"

It's Monday afternoon, five days before the state meet. I stop on a dime, forcing students to veer around me. Packs of girls in sweaters and skirts holding books in their bosoms practically knock me over. I can't move. I'm stuck. My world has shrunk to Mike and me. Jesus Himself could appear in the hallway and I wouldn't notice. As I hold my gaze on Mike, the entire season rushes by in the recesses of my mind and two words leap to the fore: *Chris Ruhl.*

Chris, my senior, the first four-year athlete I've coached. Chris, who's been running better and better, chopping chunks off his times. Chris, who can get from home plate to first base faster than any guy on the team but is still a commoner on the Holmdel trails. Chris, my sixth man.

I think of Chris because I know instantly that Gallagher has not won an award or gotten his driver's license or decided to go into the priesthood. He's Gallagher. He loses his water bottle, forgets his running shoes, cheats on his sit-ups. Though he is not a candidate for St. Rose Man of the Year or Coast Star Athlete of the Week, Gallagher has a fierceness that remains to be excavated—a battle, sad to say, I'm thus far losing with one shot left on Saturday.

Before I can utter a word, a plea to Mike in this Christian place for news that will not break my heart, the ever earnest Solebello delivers the message with solemn finality. "He went to trainer with some kind of hip problem."

Some kind of hip problem? True, there are many kinds of hip problems that runners pick up. It could be square in the hip or referred pain from the legs, buttocks, or back. It could be tendinitis coming from the knee, or more specifically an irritation to the iliotibial band that runs from below the knee to the hip area. It could be major or minor, a pain you can't walk on or something that clears up in no time.

I pepper Solebello with questions but he knows nothing other than Gallagher complained of hip pain and went to the trainer. Gallagher is not a complainer. He may look for a shortcut but he can work when he wants to. After practice, he'll put in a night as a busboy saving tips for a Mustang. But not just a Mustang, a loaded Mustang. I can picture Gallagher driving down Ocean Avenue with his elbow out the window and revving the engine to impress girls. He'd sport that great Gallagher grin like he knew something you didn't, hiding the doubts of all boys trying to break away.

I rush down the St. Rose halls, through the cafeteria, and up the stairs to Melinda's small corner office next to the gym. A tall woman who's all business and takes no nonsense from students or ogling coaches, Melinda tapes a girl's ailing foot while Gallagher sits on a metal folding chair. She says Gallagher's pain is on the right side in the low back. It feels hot and is tender to the touch so it seems like a muscle spasm. Melinda found Justin to have one leg slightly shorter than the other—a leg-length discrepancy as we runners call it—and placed a pad under his foot to even his gait. After months of running, even a quarter-inch difference can cause pain—especially in Gallagher's case since he wears his running shoes to the bone. Melinda orders ice, an anti-inflammatory and no running for a couple of days and we'll see what happens.

I tell Gallagher to "show me where it hurts." He's had the discomfort for a while but said nothing until it flared up. He ran through it. Tough but wrong. Gallagher stays with Melinda for electric muscle stimulation and I go out to practice feeling deflated. Without Gallagher, our state meet chances fade to almost zero. But I'm calculating. *Chris Ruhl, what if . . .*

Later, Melinda drives Gallagher out to the lake so he won't have to walk. She repeats that she can't tell if his problem is structural or a routine overuse injury that sooner or later almost all runners get. I have Gallagher show me again. He raises his shirt and with his thumb and index finger outlines a six-inch section of his lower back. It doesn't hurt sitting but it does hurt walking. When he brings his knee to his chest, it hurts. Run—not only run but *race*—in five days?

Kids, being young and supple, can surprise you. They heal fast. Last year, Lavender turned an ankle on our home course and had to be carried away. The next day he showed up at practice like, *Ankle, what ankle?* On the other hand, in my first year of coaching I had a boy with a back problem that wouldn't go away and he had to quit.

Seeing my concern, the team is dejected and it's a wan practice. Driving home, I grow tired from the ordeal and have to pull off the road for a nap. All season, I've longed for this time when the boys' running would carry the most meaning. Our values, character, and humanity would be put to the test. We would touch one another as never before, affirm the hard work, achieve a state of grace. This was our chance.

"Purity of soul," wrote Kierkegaard, "is to will one thing." We have been after one thing: truth. My boys are at truth's door. Truth leads to holiness. My boys have earned the privilege to get it right. Bullshit to the left, truth to the right. The boys are ready.

But I've got a runner in pain. To survive a blow like this, you rationalize. First you deny, then accept, then rationalize. The more important the mission, the greater the fall. I took that risk. I tried to create a family and relationships. When parents first picked up their sons after practice, I went right up to the cars, put my head through the windows and told the moms and dads how well the boys were doing and my hopes for them. They had a new life now, the life of the team, and the parents smiled and welcomed that and told me that at home over dinner that's what everyone talked about—the team.

We are so much a family that we take it for granted. When the parents come to meets and greet me with a "Hi, Coach," and chat about the boys, we share an enriched understanding like congregants clasping hands at the end of Shabbat services. I can't allow a fall now. Saturday could offer a new climax: perhaps something less than glory but still truth. I have to separate the two.

So Chris Ruhl it is, the possible fifth scorer to replace the ailing Gallagher, whom I doubt will run if he cannot walk. Then I think of my other senior, the runner in exile, John Lennon. He's been playing AAU basketball so he's got to be in some shape. I kept him on my official roster with the state just in case he came back. Dick Alger nixes that idea. He says it's wrong to put a boy who quit for another sport back on the cross-country team. It sets a bad precedent and is unfair to the other boys. Dick's right and I applaud his principled stand.

Of course I wouldn't be in this pickle if we didn't have the smallest team in New Jersey, if not the United States. Seven guys. I think of all the good runners I lost to soccer. Especially this kid Anthony Arnold who had running experience and ran a few of our summer practices. Never mind Rob Moore, the state track champion who plays soccer in the fall. If I had the freshman Arnold he'd probably be in Gallagher's league and I'd be sitting pretty. Everything would be the same: five good runners for state.

I put on my victim's hat, thinking, *Forget about St. Rose, the team, what am I busting my chops for—there's always something to derail my plans.* Then I come to my senses. Our team has set a record for injuries: none until now. My system of underdoing it has been working. Gallagher's injury is freakish. Maybe it'll go away as fast as it came.

When I address the team, I tell them our challenge has been made greater and we will have to respond. The boys know the performance math. They know what Bishop Eustace and Montclair Kimberley can run. They know what we can run without Gallagher. It doesn't add up for us. I remind everyone that Chris has improved his Holmdel time by a whopping two minutes this season and can run faster still. He's a senior and a four-year man with about three thousand career miles in his legs.

Chris smiles but says little. The boys respect him. They have to forget about the math. Mike Dunn says if Gallagher's not running state, he's not running. Of course. Brock's visibly upset. Last year at state he suffered stomach distress, a factor in our third-place finish. When Gallagher's dad picks him up, I give him the lowdown and he seems to doubt his son's case, insisting the boy not get any "special treatment." After they leave, I tell everyone to pray for Justin.

I call Gallagher at night to see how he's doing. The same. I remind him to ice.

Gallagher's a scrawny kid. Even with all the running, he has chicken legs. A big reason for high school injuries is an inactive childhood. No one walks anymore. Kids get driven everywhere, keeping their muscles weak and bone density low. Once they start running an ambitious cross-country program, they're sitting ducks for injuries like stress fractures. As one exercise physiologist told me, Kenyan youths, who walk and run miles to school at an early age, don't know what a stress fracture is.

To feel more in control, I search for a reason Justin got hurt. At Tuesday's practice, the boys remind me of the fall Justin took a week ago on the boardwalk. He tripped on a step but got right up and finished the workout. We laughed about his clumsiness. That could be it. But a week ago? Melinda agrees with the boys. The fall could have triggered a reaction that eventually surfaced as pain.

That's good news. Better for a specific incident to be the culprit than months of mileage. The chances are better for a faster recovery. We change the subject as Gallagher sits with an icepack while the boys stretch. Brock and Mike Solebello show pictures of their fishing trip. They caught fifty-two porgies between them. I love it when the guys shoot the bull about something like fishing. In our crazy world, it's reassuring to know that boys still go fishing with their dads.

We're tapering off this week and I have the boys run one mile easy, one mile hard, and one mile easy. It's too late to get any stronger, and the team needs to store up rest for Saturday. I just want to keep the boys' legs moving and their minds eager. I tell them we're doing just what the New York City marathoners did last week before Sunday's event. This leads Mike Dunn to claim he could outrun any woman in the marathon and to prove it he will run a marathon on a track, 105 laps, at the end of the school term in June.

Lavender's not here and the guys say he wasn't in school, either. No one knows why. His name prompts the boys to shadowbox as a joke. I ignore it and call Lavender, who tells me his family is in the middle of a social occasion for his mother and her fiancé. I don't know why this requires a day off from school but Ryan assures me he'll run on his own. I tell him he'd better show up the rest of the week or else.

I'm pushing for immortality and Lavender's not even here.

Wednesday we practice at Holmdel Park for our last look at the race course. It's almost dusk when we start running and we see five baby deer grazing on a field. I take this as a good omen and tell the boys this exquisite picture is a symbol of the beauty of cross-country and of what they can feel on Saturday.

Everyone is present, all seven boys, the full team. I begin delivering the workout and they chip in saying, "Coach, I think we need more work on the Bowl." And: "Yeah, Coach, that's been a weak spot of mine." It's a consensus. The boys volunteer, as a group, to do the hardest work. No one, not even Dunn, pleads for the easy stuff. We're together, my boys and me, seeking the same pinnacle.

Gallagher's condition is a little better and, after conferring with Melinda, we agree he can try jogging. Walking no longer hurts and when I call again at night Gallagher says he's fine but I can't tell if that's really his father talking. As a precaution, I keep Gallagher on the lower flats. He protests, asking to run the Bowl. No, but he can jog up the trail and join us in the woods when we stop and discuss strategy for the meet. I have a ton of ice for him if he needs it.

The woods circling the Bowl have a muted cast with recent apple reds and lemon yellows softening to auburn and mustard. A slice of fading sun covers the top of the hill. The setting is majestic. This spot, which two thousand teenagers will try to conquer on Saturday, is a treasure but few people can get here on foot. On the St. Rose fall sports awards night, I always tell the audience that if they want to get an idea of cross-country's arduous journey, trying *walking* the Holmdel course.

I give the boys three Bowl loops, half the usual load. I let them run quietly. They chose the workout. They know what's at stake. I stand on the side and enjoy their eagerness. "Excellent." is all I say. "Excellent."

I remind Brock and Ryan not to lead early on Saturday and that I'll be furious if I see that. I know they know but I have to say it. And it's a good thing I do. While Ryan looks a little embarrassed, as though I'm addressing him, which I am, Brock pipes up, saying, "Coach, you know I like to lead."

I'm floored. "What are you talking about? You've never been in the lead except for the easy dual meets where the competition is weak."

Brock repeats that he likes being out front as in the Keansburg meet. I tell him, "Keansburg had no one good, we took one through five against them. In the state meet there will be ten runners at your level. Do the smart thing. Work from the group. Don't expose yourself." He listens and I add, looking at both him and Ryan, "Why do you think Olympic distance races are usually slow? Because no one wants to lead. They know that they'll get run down by the pack and have no chance for a medal. This is your Olympics."

I send the team to the tennis courts and have the boys do three flat loops at a good pace but holding back. Gallagher slowly works his way up the trail to join us. As he comes into view, we wait for his assessment. Gallagher's stride looks off-kilter but he says he feels no worse after thirty minutes running so we're all encouraged by the prospect that maybe he will compete on Saturday after all. Chris Ruhl says his hamstring hurts and I don't let that faze me even though he must still play an important role at state. If Ruhl or Leschak manages to finish ahead of the fifth scorer from a key opponent, that's a net advantage for us.

We congregate on the open trail a little past two miles where it's hard to be aggressive as you marshal your strength for the kick through the woods to the finish. For my last words to the boys, I draw upon their five months of preparation going back to early summer when they were an unscrubbed group wilting in the heat.

"Remember what you guys looked like in June. Brock, you could barely move with that rear end of yours. Dunn, you couldn't finish a workout. Solebello, you were gasping. As a group, you were not in any shape, you guys were not a team, and I didn't know if we'd come close to achieving the goals we set for ourselves."

They nod, laugh, and poke fun at each other.

"You were nowhere but you worked hard, did the right thing, made many sacrifices. You sloshed through the mud against some of the best runners in the country. This is your moment. Look how far you've come. Think of how you'll feel if you let anything prevent you from reaching your goal. You are ready. And our mission is clear-cut and very simple. Run smart by holding back early, sticking with teammates, using your strength to outrun fading opponents toward the end. You know the course as well as anyone. You know how to run every section. And remember: The Bowl is your friend."

Solebello asks if I'll be at the Bowl to encourage them, saying, "That always helps me, Coach. It's like I feel tired, then you wake me up." Sure I will. "That's my favorite part, Mike, waking you up at the Bowl."

Then I deliver my mantra: "Every runner counts, every point counts, passing a single runner can make all the difference. Here, at the tennis courts, many runners give up. Not you. Push through pain. The pain is short. If you conquer it, it goes away. You enter a new world, you're on a different level, you're a different person, nothing can stop you. Look for our opponents. Pass a Montclair runner, pass a Eustace runner. Go after your teammates ahead."

We have seen that the *Star-Ledger* has tabbed Montclair Kimberley the favorite, with Bishop Eustace next and us third. "Great for us. We're not considered the favorite but we know we have the best team, right? On Saturday, in our race, people at the park will be focused on the Swede."

I say yet again that even though Brock and Ryan may be capable of matching the Swede, there's no reason to. "Go for second and third, run smart, no worse than the top five. Then we need Mike Dunn around tenth to fifteenth, Solebello in the top twenty-five." I address Gallagher as though he'll run, but I'm still not sure. "Gallagher, you try to stick with Solebello and see how that feels. Ruhl and Leschak, don't worry about place, concentrate on passing as many guys as possible, one runner at a time."

I figure around sixty points will win it. The key is Gallagher. If he's in pain, if the crunching hills cause his tender muscles to spasm, he could be one hundredth or even drop out. What else can I do but pray?

I pour out my zeal in near darkness. "Look how far we've come, look what we've overcome. Last month, we didn't practice for a week after the ocean incident. We have the smallest team in New Jersey and here we are contenders for a state title. You've done it yourselves. You've done it by recognizing your power and caring about each other."

I point to Lavender and say, "You care about Brock, don't you?" I point to every boy and do the same, pairing the boys at random. "Each of you is counting on every team member to come through. If you care about one another, if you respect one another as well as yourselves, you will."

"Coach," offers Mike Solebello, "we care about you, too."

Heads nod. I bite my lip.

"It's agreed then. We all care enough to reach our goal on Saturday."

We run easy the next two days. At school, Dick Alger calls me aside and whispers that "the fire trucks are ready." It's a St. Rose custom to honor state championship winners with a ride down Belmar's main drag in a honking fire truck. I appreciate Dick's effort but really don't care. My mind is on Gallagher. Melinda says he can run if he feels up to it. Before I can ask him, Gallagher says he's running.

"How's it feel?"

"I'm running, Coach."

I wish my wife, Andrea, could come to the state meet. She wishes I could be with her visiting Jamie at college on Saturday. We accept our divergent needs, but my coaching is still hard for her to swallow. She's no stranger to embracing kids. Andi's a terrific second-grade teacher whom parents seek for their youngsters. I can't blame her for wanting to take in a Broadway show or see the foliage in Vermont. My committed weekends strike her as separating myself from the family, which I did a decade ago, bicycling to and from the kids' soccer tournaments instead of going together, running races every other weekend, and taking elective trips to cover track events abroad. That detachment contributed to my feelings of aloneness and the turbulent pain of '94, which though long since quelled have a way of reappearing and doing damage.

Since coaching my boys in running makes me feel whole, I guess I risk letting it take over my life like my own running once did. At least now I understand the grip of things. Coaching gives me a sense of control. The more I put into it, the more the boys and I get out of it. Then the team's not only a family but one that bursts with power like a force of nature.

What control can I exercise with Dad, whose therapy cannot alter the dysfunction of his right arm and leg as he prepares to leave the rehab center and come home? Mom sticks by his side all day, and I vow to help more, to inject myself deeper into the crisis, but not yet, not until the cross-country season is over.

After a fitful sleep, I swim the morning of the meet. It's a while before I calm myself but the palliative water works and I arrive at Holmdel early to get the boys' race numbers and do my paperwork. During the morning, parking lots fill and officials line cars on the race perimeter as the site crowds to capacity. It's a partly gray day but comfortable and parents arrive with folding chairs and sit near the start, where twelve races will go off in various divisions.

I'm concerned that we'll put our stuff at a tree next to Rumson again. I don't want any little thing to throw off Lavender. It turns out Rumson runs an early race and leaves before our guys get settled. In fact, both Lavender and Gallagher are late. I wanted everyone here by ten. It's ten, where are those two guys? Now I do get nervous.

It's the state meet for crying out loud. Everyone on time. This is pristine territory, no screw-ups allowed. Lavender and Gallagher arrive at ten ten. Not good enough. Today Holmdel is our haven. We leave behind the tumult of decay that Philip Roth calls "the indigenous American berserk."

The boys' efforts will represent the best of America: bedrock values of hard work and humility, the search for higher ground, respect for effort that appears beyond reach. When they set out today on these hills, culminating months and years when they showed the courage to change and be different, they reject the corrosive elements around them, slowing the world, touching one another, and me, with their inherent goodness.

My boys inhabit a new-old universe. They look edgy because what's at stake is not something small like a trophy but the big idea of rightness, which I believe they understand in their hearts even if they cannot articulate it. How much do they really care? How much can they endure to show it? Leschak breaks the ice showing up in a white bow tie and chains, and he's the one running the best of late.

I make a point of touching each boy. A pat on the back, shaking hands, some form of physical contact. I engage each boy as an individual. The boys discuss whether they'll wear their good-luck black socks. Ryan says that since he's not been running well he won't. His father, Dennis, has flown in from Florida, where he has a condo. Dennis is in a good mood. I'm glad to see him talking easily with Ryan because they've had some tough moments. Karen Lavender is here with her fiancé. Ryan seems okay. If Ryan's okay, I'm okay.

Brock's mom, Terry, says Brock was nervous for the first time today. She describes how he spoke to her impatiently. I give him an extra touch. Mike Dunn is up. At practice, he said he would make the top ten. I doubt that but if he does we'll be hard to beat—

assuming Gallagher stays on his feet.

Gallagher looks sullen. I do not ask him how he feels. I don't want to make his injury a topic of discussion. Just forget it and run. I think *fierceness*. Gallagher's hidden fierceness. He's shown courage all week denying pain. But this is a race. Just give me eighteen minutes, man, out-think your pain for eighteen minutes.

Mike Solebello has a new job: pulling Gallagher along. If anyone is up to the task, it's Solebello. I tell him to watch for Gallagher, talk to him, help him get through the pain. "Sure, Coach." They must be a pair, working in the second tier, where unlikely heroes emerge.

Each boy is the sum of everything we've done for three years as they take the start. After stride-outs and stripping off their sweats, they gather for the "Hail Mary" prayer and Ruhl, the senior, speaks the words with conviction. The boys' faith in a higher power to guide them elevates the sense of their own value, affirming that they are worthy of divine intervention. In their recitation, they show their Catholic imprint with ideas given weight through the long journey of their choosing.

I shake every hand one more time, part with "Do what you know how to do," and head up the first hill to wait and hope.

Mater Dei's Tom Santifort, the eternal front-runner, appears first in the field of 130. His thick neck and short steps carry him upward. He won't last. Brock is second. That's my boy. He's intent, letting Santifort do the work but clinging to him when he should be relaxed.

Then Mike Dunn arrives. Dunn! Dunn in the top five. I'm shocked. This is the first time Dunn's going for it. His face shows clarity; he's never looked better. But too soon? He's ahead of the Swede, who runs easily with a Montclair Kimberley teammate at his side. Bishop Eustace has at least one boy up front. They wear yellow but so do other teams and it's hard to distinguish them. I just hope Dunn doesn't blow it Lavender-style with an early rush leading to a fizzle. I urge them on with few words but make sure they hear me above the crowd's cheers.

Lavender? Where's Lavender? How could he not be linked with Dunn? You're up, you're down. Brock up there, dependable. Dunn a surprise, running with authority. Where the hell is Lavender? Many seconds later the second pack comes: Solebello around twentieth, where he should be, with Gallagher close, sticking, sticking, showing no sign of pain, no expression, just running on memory. And with them, filling out the top twenty-five, is Lavender. What's he doing? What is he trying to pull? What could possibly be wrong with the boy after two minutes of running?

I'm running madly down the car path following the field as I make my way to the Bowl. My thoughts are a jumbled blur. I quickly compute. Okay, if Lavender bombs out, I have Dunn up there to take his place among the leaders. Assuming Dunn can hold on. What in God's name is Lavender doing so far back?

I meekly call out to him. "Look alive." That's all I can say. This is what it comes to? After three years, hundreds of practices, thousands of miles, this is what it comes to? Was my cockamamie assessment right—is the boy shoving running back in our faces?

Then a jolt. Lavender wakes up and starts moving. He leaves Solebello and Gallagher and flies down the trail passing runners one by one, not too fast, but with precision, with calculation and a committed look on his face. Now I see it. The gift from him to me—to us—in the extreme. That's Lavender, never simple or easy, never predictable, but showing me, himself, that he could finally do it. He could start from behind, conserve energy, move up, and do the job. He could use restraint, control his emotion, contain his impulse. Lavender could change.

Heading for the Bowl I see Tom Fleming, the Montclair coach and former marathon star. He fills me in on Oskar Nordenbring, and remarks that coaching is so easy. He means that if you know the training, kids' times will improve. I don't tell him I've been trying for so much more.

I risk a fall by hurtling down the leaf-covered, root-hidden shortcut to the Bowl. Before the runners appear on the ridge, the place shows off its majesty, and in the crucible of the hill, the tone for the race will be set. Who shall live and who shall die? Who shall be emboldened and who shall grow weak?

The Swede leads. I get a close look at him. He's a freshman but seems much older. Maybe it's his height or his clean carriage. He's long and lean. He takes the Bowl seamlessly as the second man appears. It's Pat Stevenson of Eustace. His jersey is lemon yellow, like the Bowl trees at their peak. I use that recognition the rest of the race, telling the boys, "Go after yellow."

Then, oh my, it's Lavender third. I gesture wildly. I'm the nut on a New York street corner talking to himself. "Perfect, perfect. Yellow. Go after yellow." I get a lump in my throat over Lavender, whom I've tried to hug into submission and now, finally, when it matters most, takes the essential lesson of running to heart. How hard it must be for him to submit. And to do it from back in the field, a stamp, as though on a passport, that this is who he is, running for the team, knowing he can come through, thwarting the need in his bones to burst out like Santifort, who now struggles, defeated, from behind.

Brock is fourth, holding his ground but lacking zest. He almost looks confused. Now I know where all that like-to-lead talk came from. He wanted to break seventeen minutes. He knew he could outrun Santifort, who recorded 16:51 a week ago and Brock whom considered a favorite. If he shadowed Santifort, he'd hit his time and maybe win the race. In his mind, there was no risk. Just follow Santifort and you're a made man.

With his rock-solid dependability, Brock has earned the right to a little wiggle room. At least he didn't actually lead. Despite his tactical lapse, I have no doubt he'll come through. Brock will make it. I know he will.

Dunn's slipped to tenth but that's okay. Better now. Settle down, boy, you knew you wouldn't place third. Now, at the Bowl, with half a race left, secure your position and don't let go. "Run with authority," I call. He knows my rap and responds like he got the message all along. "This hill is your friend."

Solebello and Gallagher hang in around twentieth and I rally them with all I have. "Beautiful. beautiful. Go after yellow. That's where the race is. The yellow guys." While Montclair has three boys well placed, the team's next two runners are far back and it looks like St. Rose vs. Bishop Eustace for the state title.

Sandwiched between Dunn and the Solebello-Gallagher tandem is the rest of the Eustace team. It's close. The scoring could go either way. Gallagher's the key. He's put us in there. I can tell he's in pain because otherwise he'd be ahead of Solebello. But Gallagher's glued to Solebello's rear. No expression, clutching for life, showing the fierceness he had all along—the fierceness I begged for.

I blast back up the shortcut with my heart in my mouth. When I reach the tennis courts, I have to stop and bend over. But I still feel relief that greatness is imminent. Ryan, Brock, Mike, Mike, and Justin united as one. Everything right as they crested the Bowl. Ruhl and Leschak, them too, denying the course, positioned well up in the field.

Here they come onto the flat, vacant loop and I beseech them. It's the same order: Oskar, the Eustace kid, Ryan, and Brock, with Mike Dunn tenth, the other Eustace boys in yellow, and Solebello and Gallagher around twentieth. This is what we talked about. The no-man's-land of the tennis courts. One mile to go.

"No letup. Go after yellow. Push through. Push through. Show you care. Don't let your teammates down. Gallagher. Mike needs you. Don't let go. Stick with it. Go after yellow. That's it. Bring it home. It's all downhill from here."

I race down the car path to the finish. Normally, I'm sluggish here, worn out, but I'm cruising, passing people, passing high school runners cheering for their teams. Glancing at the field now flying through the woods, I barely make out my boys through the trees but I can see the yellow of Eustace, still together, not giving an inch. "St. Rose," I call, barely able to get the words out in flight, "Eustace is right behind! Don't let up, you're almost there."

Reaching the slope down to the finish, which is still more than a hundred yards from me, I make out the Swede crossing first with Stevenson of Eustace second and Brock rallying to pass Ryan on the homestretch for third. As I get closer to the rope lined by spectators, I see Dunn running in tenth, well ahead of the Eustace quartet. Dunn—he's doing it for us. Dunn, running his best race ever. King Michael.

I count places and try to memorize. I have nothing to write with. I gave my clipboard to a parent. I try to compute team scores but can't keep the numbers straight. Solebello and Gallagher emerge from the woods like angels. They pump hard, together, the elegant Solebello with his lofty stride, the gallant Gallagher tighter, his mouth askew like a fighter in the tenth round. I count top twenty-five for both.

I can't tell if we've won but right now I don't care. The boys have gone through the door to a better place, and I want to crawl under a bush and cry my eyes out. Each boy has run his best. That's all I asked for.

As the boys walk through the finish chute, knees buckling, they grab one another's shoulders for balance. In the chute, life returns after the blur of racing. But the body is forced to stop abruptly when it needs to ease back to stasis. Within moments, my boys look fresh and happy, glowing in the aftermath of their deliverance. One exception: Gallagher. He's limping. I leave the boys alone to greet parents, get drinks, and cool out. I briefly shake parents' hands, and they ask if we've won. I say, "It's close. Us or Eustace."

The *Press* reporter, Mike Kerwick, runs up to me, shows me his notes, and says we won. But his calculation gives us over seventy points and I know that's wrong so I hold out for the official tally. One result is certain: Montclair Kimberley is third. Even though the team had boys fifth and sixth after the victorious Oskar, the Cougars' last two scorers were far back, showing once again that a few stars don't win but whole teams do.

The announcer begins to recite the standings. They do it Miss-America-style. If Bishop Eustace is called second, we know victory is ours. I stand with parents in a group. The boys are spread around the finish area mixing with friends. It's Mater Dei fifth with 130 points, Eastern Christian fourth with 125, Montclair Kimberley third with 78 . . . Bishop Eustace second with 66 . . . and St. Rose the winner with 56.

It's the school's first Parochial B state cross-country championship in twelve years. Dick Alger tells me the fire trucks are ready. Gee, great, Dick. Kerwick asks to interview one runner. The boys are jogging back to the start to retrieve their sweats. I tell him to find Gallagher.

When we regroup, the boys are animated but subdued compared to other winning teams. They understand the meaning of their accomplishment. They accept victory with grace, honoring their families with quiet strength. For the first time, the boys seek me out for hugs, approaching me with tentative male embraces and warm remarks. I want to tell them, *You knew it all along, didn't you, that you could run like that, and show all your best qualities at the same time,* but keep those thoughts to myself.

As they sip from water bottles, I tell each boy, all seven, "You did it for us. You helped us win," and then say something specific about their effort. Brock led the team with a consistent run up front and a late charge for third. Ryan used brilliant pacing and never let up to take fourth, assuring that our first two men were in the top five. Mike Dunn ran his best race of the season for tenth, beating all but one Eustace runner. Mike Solebello stuck with the pace, placing twentieth, remarkable for a sprinter. Justin showed tremendous courage running with pain for twenty-first, and I make a point of telling that to his father. Chris made the top fifty with another sub-twenty-minute performance. Leschak improved his time and beat half the field, and he's only a sophomore.

Oskar's winning time is 17:01. Brock and Ryan ran 17:24 and 17:29. Mike Dunn ran 17:49. Mike Solebello and Justin were almost stride for stride in 18:29 and 18:31. Chris and Leschak crossed in 19:58 and 20:34. The St. Rose team scoring: 3-4-10-19-20/47-60. The Eustace scoring: 2-14-15-17-18/21-24. Our team time was nine seconds a man faster than Eustace ran.

Waiting for the awards ceremony, I contemplate the season. The problems and lessons, the laughter and tears, the aggression and tenderness. I think about what it means when young runners finally care about their efforts—care about learning—as much as the coach, the teacher, does. Coach and athlete seeking the same thing. When that occurs, when kids respond and grow, you feel a purifying consonance and, I think, a restored faith in the promise of life itself.

We're called to the awards podium. The boys walk with humility and smile for the cameras. We get our trophy and medals. I think how wonderful it is that John Leschak, who didn't finish his first race as a freshman and almost quit the team—and who has clipped his white bow tie back on—sports a state championship medal (and various chains and chokers) around his neck.

We hurry from the park to reconnoiter at the spot outside Belmar where Dick Alger has ordered the fire truck to parade us into town. Once close by, I'm disoriented and can't quite find the place. Finally, when I think I've got it, I'm in an office parking lot off a highway. No one's here. No parents, no boys, no Dick. No fire truck. I must be in the wrong place.

I head for town's main street. I worry that Dick will be upset not seeing me. I can still jump on the fire truck as it moves past Freedman's Bakery and Pat's Tavern to the school. Hokey St. Rose traditions like this are oddly comforting, and I collapse on a bench awaiting the team's jubilant arrival. But still no team, no parents, no truck. Finally, Dick appears and says the signals were crossed, the fire truck's not coming after all, and he sent everybody home. It's just as well.

I sit sleepy on a bench on the main street devouring a container of rice from the Chinese takeout as the fall sun blurs and a chill gathers. I think about my boys, mainly Lavender, who talked about having a party tonight and asked me to stop by. I had to say no, I have to get back to my family. I consider how Lavender persevered and the endurance he showed, an endurance that defined our quest. Lavender showed me qualities I hope I can live up to, and I realize they all did that, these innocent and beautiful boys, in the end teaching me, coaching me, clearing a path for me in some cosmic, interlocking way.

With their knowing mistakes and teenage abandon, alternating sparks of brilliance with wicked delights, they seemed to know all along that the true path to greatness had to have detours and embody a kind of imperfect balance because that's what life's made of. They moved from naïfs to conquerors with a personal assurance that eluded me but was a part of their genius, the arrogant genius of youth. From the start, I suspected these boys were better than me, had more to give, and now I know as I take from them and try to march on with a lighter load and safer feelings about the world around me.

I feel I've done good coaching these boys, these Catholic boys, a calling from my Jewish soul. They should know how they've blessed me. Michael Dunn, Justin Gallagher, Ryan Lavender, John Leschak, Chris Ruhl, Brock Silvestri, Michael Solebello. These boys, my heroes.

Postscript

All of the 2000 team members, except for senior Chris Ruhl, who went on to college, returned for the fall 2001 cross-country season, and St. Rose repeated as state champions in the Parochial B division. The results were almost identical to the previous fall: We again scored 56 points, while runner-up Bishop Eustace had 68, compared with 66 in 2000. But our team was not the same in attitude or disposition. The boys matured in every way, took on the stature of champions, and were confident of a second state victory. At practice, they could predict my workouts and oftentimes they practically coached themselves, a tribute to their zest for learning and pride in becoming more complete athletes. I found the five key runners—seniors Michael Dunn, Justin Gallagher, Ryan Lavender, Brock Silvestri, and Michael Solebello—very much my equals in making a commitment to excellence. We were in the same huddle from day one of 2001. The boys thrived on being outside the norm. Lesson accomplished.

Brock and Ryan led the team, alternating as top performer from one meet to the next. Ryan placed second and Brock third in our state championship run. They improved their times at the hilly Holmdel Park 5K racecourse. Brock ran 16:53 and Ryan 16:55, joining the coveted sub-17:00 club. Michael Dunn improved his time and placed eighth at state, again the critical position that secured our victory. King Michael! Justin, this time in one piece, was again our fifth scorer at state. Mike Solebello improved his best time by twenty-three seconds and had one of the best seasons any sprinter could hope for in cross-country.

John Leschak left St. Rose to attend a public school. No surprise there. John needed more room to breathe. He did some running, but put more energy into academics and made National Honor Society. I was thrilled to write out a recommendation on his behalf.

Two young runners joined the team in '01. Anthony Arnold, who'd stuck with soccer as a freshman, came out as a sophomore. Anthony may have had more potential than anyone I coached. He was our fourth scorer at state, and went on to become the team's top runner as a junior and senior, and one of the best in the conference. Christian Capron, a freshman whose main sport was swimming, also joined us. He improved all season and, with another small seven-man roster at St. Rose, Chris had the opportunity to compete in the state championships, earning a first-place medal as a freshman, as Leschak had done before him as a soph. Chris started his senior year in the fall of 2004.

In addition to our state triumph, St. Rose won the 2001 Class B Central dual-meet conference title with a 7-0 record. The boys used most dual meets as practice. They could formulate their own strategies, and they helped one another without provocation. I needed only to remind them about what they knew.

No one ran into the sea. No midrace fisticuffs. I coached young men.

Ryan Lavender went on to Rutgers University. After a year he transferred to Florida Atlantic—Ryan, still lifeguarding, always followed the sun—but he returned to New Jersey after a year and was still figuring out his college plans. Ryan has continued running on his own.

Brock Silvestri went to the University of Connecticut, where he ran cross-country and track but was injured on and off. After two years he transferred to Stockton College in South Jersey for its physical therapy program. He's running cross-country and track.

Michael Dunn, one of the top students at St. Rose, attends Boston College. Michael Solebello is a student at Quinnipiac University in Connecticut. Chris Ruhl attends Brookdale College in Monmouth County, New Jersey, taking courses in a combined program with Rutgers that enables him to work parttime. Justin Gallagher started at Brookdale, then left school to work fulltime. John Leschak attends the College of New Jersey in Trenton and made Dean's List, majoring in law and justice. Anthony Arnold started CNJ in fall 2004 and is a recruit on the cross-country and track teams.

John Lennon, Sgt. Pepper, went on to Washington College in Maryland, on a basketball scholarship, and has begun his senior year. He and his family suffered the loss of John's father, John "Jay" Lennon, a Port Authority police officer who perished while attempting to rescue victims during the World Trade Center attacks of September 11, 2001.

My father, Martin, showing more courage than even a cross-country runner, has managed well, walking tentatively with a cane, with help from my mother and a home health aide—and our entire family. Living close by, I am able to see them often and have found ways to lower my guard and be closer emotionally. My older daughter, Allison, has a child of her own—our granddaughter—who lifts the spirit of everyone in her midst including my parents, now great-grandparents.

As for my coaching, I gave up my St. Rose position after the 2001 fall season. I felt I'd done all I could with the team and, after five years, needed to spend more time with my wife, tend to my parents, and run more miles myself. It was time to put away my fraying coach's accordion folder; eventually, I'm sure I'll pick it up again.

Teachers say the best thing about education is when a former student, by deed or accomplishment or perhaps by returning to school to pay you a visit, demonstrates that your work did some good. I was blessed with immediate feedback when Michael Dunn dropped off the following letter, framed, at my home shortly after the 2001 cross-country season.

Afterword

Letter presented to the coach that was written for a college application, by Michael Dunn, in his senior year.

Throughout my life there have been several people who have had a significant influence on me. One that comes to mind is Marc Bloom. I met Marc the summer before my freshman year. I was at an orientation for St. Rose High School. I walked into the cafeteria, where the school's different athletic teams were urging incoming freshmen to sign up. Before I could even glance at any other table, the coach of the boys' cross-country team scurried up to me. "You look like a good runner," Marc said to me. Now at that time, I was about four feet eleven and a hundred pounds, and thinking back, I realize that I could not have possibly looked like a good runner. But Marc's words worked. This energetic man had sparked something inside me, and I signed up for the cross-country team.

I am now a senior and captain of the cross-country team. This man whom I had met four years earlier was right. I am a good runner. Throughout the four years I have known Coach Bloom, his persistent work ethic has inspired me greatly. Last year, early in the cross-country season, I began to slack off. I was not working to my potential, and it was showing in my running. One day at practice, my teammates and I decided to skip our running and go swimming in the ocean. To try to get out of trouble, we lied about it. The next day, Coach Bloom found out about it. He wasn't mad that we went swimming instead of running. What really hurt him was the fact that we had tried to deceive him. As he spoke to the team about what we had done, I saw raw emotion in his eyes. He was deeply upset. A few days later, he spoke to me in private and told me that if I would just get serious, I could still have a great season.

I decided to work hard for the remainder of the fall season, and run with more determination. I slowly improved. After our team won the Parochial B State Championship, Coach Bloom told me I had run the best race of my life and that he was proud of me. Once again I saw the emotion in his eyes, but this time his eyes expressed joy. Our team victory in the state meet led to an appearance in *Runner's World* magazine. In the article, Marc wrote about the meet, "I'm so proud of these guys . . . that I don't care if we've won. I just want to crawl under a bush and cry my eyes out." It was the truth. You could see it in his face as he talked to us.

Marc Bloom has encouraged me to strive for my goals both in cross-country and in life. He has shown me through his words and actions what a truly dedicated person is. He is an example to me, because now I aspire to be ambitious and diligent. Last summer, I attended the St. Rose freshman orientation to help out. Coach Bloom couldn't make it, so I took his place at the boys' cross-country table where I had met him four years earlier. While I was persuading upcoming freshmen to join the squad, I spotted a young boy of small stature observing the different sports' presentations. I walked up to him and said, "You look like you could be a good runner. You should think about joining the cross-country team."

As I spoke those words, I thought back to the years I had been under the guidance of Coach Bloom. I realized that I now had the ability to inspire this young boy in much the same way that Marc Bloom had inspired me.